# THE BEGINNER'S COMPLETE KARTING GUIDE

## by Jean Louis Genibrel

ISBN 0-936834-40-4

**Editor:** Steve Smith

**Associate Editor:** Georgiann Smith

**Cover:** Martin Teixeira

Revised July 1996

Manufactured and printed in USA

Published by

STEVE SMITH
AUTOSPORTS
PUBLICATIONS

P.O. Box 11631/Santa Ana, CA 92711/(714) 639-7681

# About The Author

Jean Louis Genibrel, a native of France, moved to the United States in 1963. His racing career started in 1968 with an Austin Healey Sprite which he raced in slaloms and SCCA races

Since then Jean has driven and built several record holding and championship cars and karts. His successes cover NASCAR, SCCA, IKF and, as a mechanic, IMSA, USAC and SCCA.

Genibrel also worked for Dan Gurney's All American Racers during the Bobby Unser era as a mechanic and fabricator, and he is a lap record holder at Ascot Park Speedway in Gardena, California in the stock heavy class.

# Dedication

This book is dedicated to:

Steve Smith, for his trust and patience.
Dale Parent, for imparting his time, talents and knowledge.
Robert Cross, for his willingness to help.
Tommy Pierson, for his continuous, undemanding
    assistance.
Tom Pierson, for his role in the start of karting.

# Thanks

A special thanks to: Jon Pierson, K&P Manufacturing; Walt Meyers, Meyers Race Engines; Bob Kindoll, Kindoll Race Engines; Chuck Pittenger, Pitts Performance; Robbie Watts, Invader Karts; Tom Patronite, Azusa Engineering; Doug Stokes, IKF; Ron Emmick and Gary Emmick, Emmick Karts; Tom Cassidy, GEM Products; Tom Wilcox and Randy Coons, Motive Systems; Doug Henline, Proline Karts; Bill Peacock, Karttech; Ron Black, KIC; Carvin Shoenberger; Burris Tire Co.; Yamaha Motors Inc.; Nippondenso Spark Plug Co.; K&N Air Filter Co.; Dick Guldstrand; Jay Dunton.

**Jean Louis Genibrel**

# Table Of Contents

# Notice

# Introduction

Welcome to the exciting world of karting, and congratulations for buying this book. It is the best few bucks you will ever spend in your racing career. This book was written with the beginner in mind, and, as a recent beginner myself, I can guarantee that this money you just spent will go a long way in savings on unneeded parts, tools, accessories, maintenance, and part failures due to lack of knowledge.

In motor racing, probably more than any other sport, knowledge is the most important factor in success. Had I known, in the beginning, that leaning the fuel/oil mixture to 50 to 1 leads to engine failure, I would not have lost a race and I would have saved ten or twelve times the cost of this book alone in engine work. Had I known that running a soft rubber compound on a dry dirt track leads to tire chunking, well, I would have finished first instead of fourth, and, saved myself fifty bucks for a new tire.

I wish, also, to congratulate you for choosing karting as a means of entering the motor racing field. You will find karting is relatively safe, inexpensive, family-oriented and can be enjoyed by young and not-so-young alike. Several "big time" drivers started in go karting (Eddie Cheevers, Al Unser Jr., Lake Speed, Ricardo Patrese, Mike Andretti, Joe Ruttman, Jodi Schechter, Swede Savage, Rene Arnoux, Bobby Unser Jr. and probably the great majority of the current FI drivers).

A kart requires minimum space to be worked on and stored, upkeep is minimal, tires last fairly well, entry fees and club dues are low, and there are local races weekly. Again, everything is relative, yet one can start kart racing on a thousand dollars, when the cheapest form of auto racing will cost five or ten times as much to start!

My favorite reason for starting out in karting is that the sport has a unique way of equalizing the competition and maintaining even and fair competition by using strict weight and engine formulas.

Karting is a drivers' form of racing. Karts are relatively uncomplicated; one gear, one carburetor, no suspension to speak of, and aerodynamics are negligible (except for Enduro and Super Kart). You can concentrate on one thing — driving. The things learned with the few setups necessary on a kart will serve you as a base for your racing endeavors.

So learn how to drive and win safely. Learn the basic setups with the tires, spindle heights, drivers weight distribution, carburetor settings, pipe lengths, wheel offsets, the role of the chassis in handling, etc.

This book is not intended to get you to Indy. This book's intent is to get you to your first kart race safely, economically, professionally, and to teach a novice the basics that would normally take months or years to learn.

In these pages you will learn how to choose a kart, and set it up for the first race. You will also find charts and lists to remind you of what to do and when. Most importantly, this volume will give you knowledge otherwise reserved for the more experienced racers and the pros. Most of those items are normally learned through experience. Other bits of knowledge are often passed on as common knowledge, when in fact they are nothing more than wives' tales. Cutting fact from fallacy is what separates the winners from the also-rans.

You are starting on the right step.

# 1
# Getting Started

If karting is good enough for Al Unser Jr., Mike Andretti, Nelson Piquet, Emerson Fitipaldi, Eddie Cheevers and probably 90 percent of the current Formula One drivers, well, karting can't be that bad a place to start a racing career.

Karts are probably the best way of getting your feet wet in 4-wheel motor racing. Karts are relatively safe, inexpensive to operate and can be transported to the track on pickups or even cars, and they can be worked on in very limited space.

Other forms of motor racing require drivers to take full physical exams with eye examination and blood type identification. Even though this is not required by any karting associations, that I know of, I still recommend a good checkup, especially if you are over 35, out of shape, and/or just came out of a serious illness. The heart should take special attention. Karting is not a physical sport, but when the adrenalin starts flowing, the heart rate goes up, and that can lead to trouble. Have your eyes (and if applicable, your glasses) checked. Better athletes, such as in football, soccer, baseball, basketball, and motor racing, have better-than-average vision, and better peripheral vision. It is also good to have your blood type verified and embroidered on your suit. Also print it on your helmet and on a medical bracelet. Include a list of any allergies and the date of your last tetanus shot. Chances are that it was in the military or high school that you had your last shots. Tetanus immunization is a good idea to get, and have the date of inoculation listed on your medical bracelet and helmet. The most important pre-

Although these lads race on a very limited budget they are always top contenders. Karting is a great training ground for young racers.

Speedway four cycle juniors offer an introduction to karting, beginning at seven years of age, and ranging in various classes up to 16 years old.

*Having your name and blood type on your suit and helmet is a good idea. This should be a rule.*

*Four cycle classes are ideal breeding grounds for future champions. Notice cut out gas tank to provide tire clearance. (Below) The four cycle classes offer a young person a real taste of competition.*

ventive measures are: blood type, heart check, full physical and eye check. You and only you can decide if you are fit to drive at high speeds around other competitors and non-movable objects you could collide with.

At this stage you must determine which form of karting you wish to start with — enduro, sprint or speedway. Speedway and sprints, I feel, should be your two choices. One might find this choice interesting coming from an ex-road racer, but remember that this book is aimed at helping you get started the cheapest and safest way possible.

The following list should help you decide which form of karting you wish to enter:

1) your age
2) your budget
3) your experience
4) the amount of time you have available to travel and work on the kart
5) long-range goals

Looking more deeply into the five points above, we find that:

**Age** is almost immaterial in karting. There are classes for juniors and there is no real limit on how old you can be to race go karts. Only you can decide based on your health and physical shape.

**Budget.** This one will separate the Smiths' from the Jones'. There is a saying in racing: "Speed costs money, how fast do you want to go?" Sprint or speedway will definitely cost less than an enduro program to operate. An enduro program will cost three to four times what a sprint or speedway show will cost. Only you can decide how much you can afford. One is better off racing speedway or sprints and do well, maybe even win a championship, and not have to

mortgage his house, rather than racing a more expensive class and do poorly because of lack of funds. There is nothing worse in racing than missing an event because of lack of money. My recommendation is for you to first decide how much you can afford per month on your racing endeavor, and then buy the appropriate equipment and stay

*Karting's growing number of racing ladies add an extra touch of class to the sport. This pretty lady has shown the guys the fast way around the track at Indian Dunes more times than we would like to admit.*

within your budget. If a new fandangle pipe comes out, resist the temptation, and buy it later when you will have a few races and a bit of experience under your belt. Spend money on necessities. Things like fancy driving suits, paint jobs, wings (which I feel are more than worthless, I feel they are downright dangerous, in sprints and speedway, and I feel they should be banned) are out. Remember that this book was written to get you through your first few races. That new pipe, those new wide tires, will probably cut your times down a few ticks. But we are only learning right now. We are building a foundation. Save those pennies; they will be better spent later when you know exactly where to spend them. I understand it is difficult to resist those tempting ads. (I was the only driver that night at Ascot, in my second race, on the pole, without a driving suit. If someone had walked up to me at the starting line and asked me to trade a driving suit for my pole position, I probably would have laughed him right off the track!) Doing well in racing makes you feel good on the inside, looking "cool" makes you feel good on the outside. Just remember that looking cool is one thing, real cool is winning.

At this point, let me warn you about "salesmanship." This word is encountered in every business, but in motor racing it can take a very costly tone. Remember that kart shop owners are in business to make money and it is easy for some of them to get over-zealous in trying to help you with things that you don't really need. In the very beginning I dealt with as many as five different shops at the same time and I checked their stories against each other. This required considerable tact in not letting the shop owners know what I was doing. By doing this I soon found the "doers" from the "talkers."

Be aware, also, of the bait and switch artists. They advertise a low price for a kart, engine or other parts. When you get to their shop and show them the ad that brought you in, they will tell you that that item has been sold out but they have another one in stock similar to the one you inquired about. At a higher price, of course. They might tell you that the kart you inquired about does not handle well anyway and the one he has was last year's champion. **Buyer Beware.**

Use this list as a shopping list and a cost guide:

| | *Approx. Cost* |
|---|---:|
| 1 used kart with spares and stand | $1100.00 |
| 2 files | 10.00 |
| 1 oil tray | 10.00 |
| 1 starter and battery | 150.00 |
| 1 set of tools | 200.00 |
| 1 drill motor | 35.00 |
| 1 gas can | 15.00 |
| 1 helmet | 100.00 |
| 1 pair of gloves | 25.00 |
| Lubricants, solvents, paint, cleaners, brake fluid, air filter spray, grease, hand cleaner | 25.00 |
| 2 sets of numbers | 8.00 |
| 1 tire pump | 12.00 |
| 1 flashlight | 10.00 |
| 1 fire extinguisher | 15.00 |
| 1 rule book | 4.00 |
| 2 sets of tear offs | 6.00 |
| 1 tire pressure gauge | 25.00 |
| 2 sets of tie wraps | 10.00 |
| Miscellaneous nuts and bolts and washers, fasteners | 20.00 |
| Clutch oil | 10.00 |
| 1 clutch puller | 7.00 |
| 1 clutch tool | 7.00 |
| 1 roll of safety wire | 10.00 |
| 1 clipboard and paper | 3.00 |
| 1 notebook | 2.00 |
| 1 compression gauge | 10.00 |
| 1 tape measure | 3.00 |
| 1 roll of duct tape | 7.00 |
| 1 chain breaker | 16.00 |
| 3 feet of chain | 12.00 |
| 2 clutch linings | 18.00 |
| 1 spark plug | 3.00 |
| Assortment of exhaust springs | 4.00 |
| 4 exhaust pipe flex | 12.00 |
| 2 gears | 25.00 |
| 25 pounds of ballast | 15.00 |
| 1 kart stand | 50.00 |
| Drivers clothing | 40.00 |
| Miscellaneous | 100.00 |

For enduro racing, figure twice as much for the kart. Dual engine machines are obviously more yet. For sprints and speedway, my figures come to about $2,000 just to get to your first race.

A tow car will cost at least a couple grand to get something decent. Just remember that you cannot drive a kart to the track.

If those figures seem prohibitive, consider a partner-

*(Left) A novice's first season's worth of trophies. Use common sense and you too can furnish your mantelpiece with some shiny stuff in your first season.*

The "Duffy" award is the highest award obtainable in U.S. karting. The "Duffy" has been dubbed the "Oscar" of karting and rightfully so. It was named after Duffy Livingstone, one of the founders of the sport of karting.

Three generations of this family have been involved in karting.

Just give him time.

ship. But, hold it right there! Racing partnerships almost never work. No matter how good intentions are in the beginning, someone always seems to get the short end of the stick. If you do enter a partnership, write down your intentions with your partner, how finances will be handled and who will have what duties. Do keep track of how much money either of you has already spent on the project (this book for instance). Know the person you are dealing with. Someone you have just met at the track just will not do.

**Experience.** If you have raced cars, go karts or motorcycles, consider enduros. Enduro karting is a good stepping stone into formula racing. Several big time drivers started in enduros. This form of racing will teach you the basics of driving, engine building, gearing, aerodynamics and racing team organization. Frankly I am not very experienced with enduro racing. I wrote this book with the budget racer in mind and I still feel that sprint and speedway are a better way of entering the field, especially for a complete neophyte. If you still wish to run enduros, I would suggest you run a few sprints or speedway races just to "cut your teeth" and in a few months, trade up to an enduro machine. By then you will know who to buy from and your dealer will perhaps be able to give you a good deal on a new enduro kart (perhaps even partial sponsorship).

**Time available.** This is rather self-explanatory. Ask around and see how much time other guys spend on their equipment. Be sure to ask the front runners, because they will usually have the cleaner, better prepared machines that require more attention and time. If you want to run in front you will have to spend at least as much time on your kart as

they do. At first you will probably spend even more time, simply because you are not used to all the different operations. You will spend some time doing some chores over and over and you will probably wish to set up some things to suit you better, such as your seat, pedals and steering height. Personally, in the beginning, I spent fifteen to twenty hours a week on my "Supersprint." After a year I am down to five or six hours per week. That includes phone calls, chasing parts and chatting at the kart shop.

A good relationship with your supplier is important to a good race program development. Your feedback is what will make next year's karts better. While at the shop, exchange ideas, but don't get in the "B.S." rut. One last thing — you will need a place to store your kart and to work on it. If you already have a garage or you can use a friend's (remember those partnerships, borrowing can lead you into the same hole), you are OK. Keep the cost of a garage in your budget because even a one-car garage can run into some money.

Now you are ready to decide if you want to go speedway, enduro or sprint racing. You might not even know the difference between those three types of karting. Briefly, they are:

**Speedway** is run on dirt oval tracks of 1/8 to 1/4 mile. Surfaces are usually sand or clay.

Both long and short track offer plenty of excitement. The longer tracks, like the 1/4-mile, require different driving techniques and kart set-ups. On a short track you can get away with more, both in your driving and the preparation of your kart. On an 1/8-mile track you can get sideways, get away with it and have fun. The 1/4-mile requires more precise driving because speeds can get as high as 70 to 75 miles per hour. The driver must use finesse and drive very smoothly to get every ounce of speed out of his machine. One must also use extra caution at those speeds because if you catch a wheel, you will wind up in the hospital in a hurry. On a short track there is more shoving and banging, mainly because the track is so much smaller and everybody is dashing for that "magical inside line."

I would suggest you start on an 1/8-mile track. You will be safer and you will enjoy your first race better.

Dirt racing does get muddy and dusty. So, be ready with tear offs and some water to clean your helmet and face shield. (Actually the trick is to let the other guys go out and get all muddy and dry out the track for you, then run the second practice.)

**Sprints** are usually run on an asphalt course with both right and left-hand turns, although several races are now held on asphalt ovals. What's great is that some of these races offer prize money.

One drawback I see to sprints is that tires wear out very fast and cost so much money. A set of asphalt track tires will last one or two races, while dirt tires will last a season on the right side (and you can then run your left side tires on the right the next year).

**Enduros** are run on sports car tracks such as Laguna Seca, Long Beach, and Riverside. These races are often held in conjunction with major events such as the Long Beach Grand Prix. "Sit ups" (sprint- or speedway-style karts) are sometimes run on those road courses too. Those races are a good way to move your way up into enduros and give you a feel of big time racing. The best way for you to decide which way to go is for you to attend some races and make your decision. Now, when you go to those races, spend all your time in the pits and ask a lot of questions. Be sure to tell your victims that you are thinking about buying a kart. The reason

Enduro karts                                    Courtesy of IKF

Speedway karts                    Courtesy of IKF

Left and above, sprint karts                    Courtesy of IKF

is that some racers are very closed mouthed, sometimes, in fear of letting their competition in on their secrets. Saying that will sometimes loosen them up. Bring a note pad and start writing. You might as well get used to this, because record keeping is a source of knowledge, and if you recall from my Introduction: "In motor racing, probably more than any other sport, knowledge is the most important factor to success." Write down names, brands, phone numbers and everything else you hear. Chances are that a lot of what you hear will conflict with what you will read in this book. That's good. If everybody in racing did the same thing there would not be a race. However, I have spent countless hours researching the karting field, and I feel that if you took the time to buy this book you should follow what this book says. Compare your notes with what I wrote. You will find, I am sure, that the front runners do things close to the way I say to do things.

Now is a good time to ask what size gear, what length pipe and which exhaust system they use. Those three things are probably the most closely kept secrets by the front runners. The exhaust system is usually obvious to most people. I still have to ask and I still sometimes get two different answers from two different crew members on the same team. But they will probably be honest with you. So note their answers and when you run against them, you will not have to ask about their gear or their exhaust systems. They will have forgotten you were the greenhorn who was asking all the questions a month or two ago. They might come and ask you questions now.

## What Classes To Start In

For a beginner there are four good possibilities: 1) The stock four cycle classes offer an inexpensive, relatively safe and trouble-free form of racing. 2) If the karter wishes more speed, a dual engine or open four cycle kart could be raced. 3) The two cycle classes: The Yamaha KT 100 has proven very reliable and inexpensive to operate. The two cycle classes range from the mild mannered restricted rookie class to the wide open 135cc class. 4) The new "US 820" class run both by IKF and WKA also offers an ideal entry level situation. The "Westbend" motor used in this class is very reliable and slower than the other two cycles, so the novice can concentrate on one thing — learning the ropes. The "spec" tire rule and the limitations on the engine means that the cost will be greatly reduced compared to the other classes. Tires should last a season and the engine does not require any machining!

*Nice looking kart and driver's uniform.*

# 2
# Buying A Kart

By now you should know whether you want to run speedway, sprints or enduros. But how do you choose your equipment? Who do you buy from? What do you look for? Where are the kart shops located? Am I buying a legal machine? Is the engine legal? What do the different classes mean?

First locate your nearest kart shop and browse around. Second, check out what is for sale on his bulletin board, and get a copy of *Karter, World Karting* or *Karttech* for their classified ads. Next go to some races and look for "for sale" signs. Fourth, ask around. Remember to look for a kart suited for the form of racing you want to compete in. For instance, an enduro kart just will not do in speedway or sprints or vice versa. Also, try to find a kart that was used in the same form of racing you intend to run. There are several reasons for that. First, the tires will be the right type. Second, spares will be suited to the form of racing you wish to enter - such as pipes, exhaust system, flex, gears, fairing for speedway. Plus you can pick the brain of the fellow you are buying the kart from for that particular form of racing.

**Buying A Used Kart.** The first thing to look at is the general condition of the kart. Is the frame painted? Is paint worn or chipped? Is welding professional? Is the kart clean? Are any damaged parts patched with bailing wire or tape? Is the seat or fairing patched with fiberglass? Just look for the general condition. A clean, good looking kart will not necessarily be a good machine for you, but a kart that looks like it has been through a war will probably give you nothing

but troubles and may be unsafe to race. Also consider what you are getting in spares and accessories. I have listed costs of accessories and spares on a previous page. Use that as a guideline to estimate the value of what you are being offered. Ideally get your kart from someone who is abandoning karting altogether. You will probably inherit his spares, accessories, leathers, helmet and other goodies, all in one good price.

The other advantage to buying a "clean" kart for a beginner is that clean karts usually belong to front runners and the information you get from a front runner is much more valuable than from the guys bringing up the rear. Do

*This speedway kart looks really clean and nice. It would be a good buy as a used kart.*

not be afraid to ask questions — lots of questions. The guy will be eager to answer because he wants to sell you his kart. So pick his brain all you can. Stay away from karts with overly done fairings or wings (except for enduros). Wings and the like do not belong on go karts. Those things are used to make go karts look like something they are not. Wings make go karts look like toys and are dangerous. And, wings are non-functional, can be dangerous, they add dead weight and are just another thing to go wrong and cost money. The danger is that they are subject to too much vibration and fall off too easily. Also, in a wreck the sharp edges offer more areas to get hurt on.

## Guidelines For Used Kart Buying

**Legality.** The best I can tell you is to study the rule book until you know it by heart. Some karts are perfectly legal for some forms of racing and in certain parts of the world. Don't buy a kart to find out that it is only legal in Europe for the world championship.

If you want to run enduros, get an enduro kart. If you want to run sprints get a sprint kart. Actually what kind of kart to buy should be dictated by the following thought: Buy what is currently winning. I have seen some guys who tried to save a few bucks on a "passe" machine thinking they could bring it back to competitive shape only to find themselves spending more money than they would have by purchasing a new or slightly more expensive kart. With the advent of wide and sticky tires, the karts have drastically changed in just a year, and last year's frames are not necessarily tomorrow's winners. Have a good idea of what you want before you start shopping.

**Clutch.** See that the clutch is suited to the form of racing you are about to enter. For sprints and speedway, the most widely used clutch is the Horstman. This clutch is the most hassle-free and it is easy to adjust. For enduros, the Bystrom seems to be the best for a beginner, mainly because of its ease of adjustment and carefree maintenance.

**Tach, Temp Gauge.** A tach and/or temp gauge will bring up the value of a kart considerably. Consider that a new tach-temp gauge combination costs almost two-hundred dollars new. The most widely used gauge is the "Digitron" unit. The DT 6E is the latest tach-temp gauge combination. The illuminated models are another fifty dollars. You will need the light if you run night races.

**Engine.** For a beginner there is absolutely no doubt, that the Yamaha engine should be the choice. This motor is dead-reliable and it is inexpensive to repair. Tuning is simple, parts are readily available, and it is competitive with the more expensive European motors. Yamaha also puts out a nifty owner's manual for just a few bucks.

Next, find out if the engine is stock. If not, find out exactly what was done to it and by whom. If the guy tells you that he and his buddy decided to "hog out" the ports after a couple six packs, well, stay away from that motor. Again, the

modified classes are for the more advanced racers. However, if you find a motor that can be brought back to stock fairly inexpensively, go for it.

*Tach and temp gauge is essential if you are going to get serious about your racing. A temperature gauge is good insurance against running too lean and sticking your motor.*

**Tires.** Look at the tire conditions and the compound. First find out what the latest compound is. Not that the compound will make a big difference your first time out, but it does have a bearing on the price. The type of tire is actually more important than the compound. For instance, a dirt tire will be useless if you want to run sprints and vice versa.

**Front End.** Before buying a kart take a quick look at the front end. See if the rod ends have a lot of slop in them and double check that nothing is bent or has been heated and bent back in place.

**Rear Axle Assembly.** Spin the rear wheels and look for friction in the wheel bearings. While rear assembly is spinning, look at the axle to see if it is bent or damaged. Now look at the drive sprocket and look for worn teeth. A chain guard is a big plus here.

**Gas Tank.** An aluminum gas tank is more desirable than a "Tupperware" tank. Some of the tanks floating around are nothing more than automotive water recovery tank. Anyhow, those tanks are nice because they let you see the fuel level. If the price is right, go for it.

**Fiberglass.** Look for cracks and signs of abuse. See if the paint will need to be redone.

**Brakes.** Hydraulic brakes are the only ones you should consider. Again, brakes are a bit trendy. See what is being run and stick to the major brands. Brakes are fairly cheap and easy to repair, but be sure the system is safe before going out on the track.

**Accessories.** The more spares and accessories you can get with a used kart, the better off you will be. The most desirable accessories are: starter, kart stand, gears, flex, exhaust pipes, ballast and driver's clothing. Spares: clutch linings, piston, ring, throttle cable, numbers, clutch oil,

*Wings are useless at most sprint and speedway races. In case of a crash those sharp edges can be very dangerous.*

engine oil, plugs, fasteners, exhaust springs.

Again, if you can find someone who is abandoning karting completely you will probably inherit all kinds of odds and ends. Remember that clothing and helmet may be hard to fit from one driver to another.

**Buyer Beware.** An educated shopper is a smart shopper and that goes for everything, not just go karts. See what is winning, and buy a kart in good shape; trying to nickel-and-dime a kart will drive you crazy and you will end up spending more money in the long run. Learning in the first year is the goal, not spending your time playing fixer-upper at the track.

**Buying A New Kart.** If you decide on a new kart (possibly the cheapest proposition in the long run), first decide the form of racing you wish to compete in, the class, the weight classification, the engine and then see what is winning. Also consider parts availability and cost. The foreign karts are much more expensive to buy and repair. If your local dealer carries a make that is not quite as strong a runner as the one you would prefer, I would still buy the kart your dealer carries based on parts and information availability.

# 3
# Accessories, Clothing, Tow Vehicle, Spares

It has been said that racing is 99 percent boredom and one percent terror. Whoever said that probably meant that it seems you spend 99 percent of your time wrenching, cleaning, sanding, welding, bolting, painting, inflating, drilling, riveting, taking notes, analyzing notes and dusting trophies. The one percent you spend at the track, worrying about what is going to break or what the competition is going to come up with next, and what you should come up with before them.

Maintenance can certainly be a grind. However, there is one thing that can make your work easier — good tools. Good tools do not mean a toolbox the size of a motorhome. Good tools does not mean cubic money, or necessarily brand names such as Proto, Mat-Co, Snap-On or whatever brand. At the beginner's stage, good tools mean tools you need and the tools that will serve their purpose when you need them. At this time good tools means the right tools — if you need a chisel, use a chisel, not a screwdriver. If you need a hammer, use a hammer, not a ratchet. What I am trying to say is, get the tools you need. The inset will show you the basic tools you should buy to get your started.

There are a few special tools you will need:

**A Good Tire Pump.** I haven't found much in that area. I guess the $15.95 ones at K Mart are just as good as any others. At that price you ought to get a couple and save one as a spare.

**Tire Pressure Gauge.** Do not skimp on a tire gauge. Get a good quality dial-type gauge, with an air pressure release valve and an end you can easily stick on the tire stem. The pencil-type gauges are not accurate enough and do not have a pressure release valve.

**Drill Motor.** 3/8-inch drive reversible, with variable speed would be nice, but just a bsic 3/8-inch drive drill will get you started.

**Drill Bits.** Be sure they are metal bits, not wood bits. Sears number 9HT67184 will do to start.

**Gas Can.** One and one-half gallons is perfect if you run a single motor class. Get the square kind — they are easier to carry to the track. If you already have a gas can check if it is clean and that it does not leak. Also your can should be equipped with a screw-on hose to dispense the fuel.

**Ratio Rite.** Those are graduated containers with markings in cc's, ratio, liters and ounces. They are used to measure oil before it is poured into the fuel. (If you run a two cycle, of course.) Ratio Rites are available at most kart shops.

**Clutch Tools.** If you run a clutch, you will need a clutch puller and a holding tool, also available at your kart shop for a few bucks. These tools are very important. Never attempt to remove your clutch without them or you may end up with a warped clutch housing (see clutch rebuilding section).

If you are going to run speedway, get a good flashlight. Speedway events are often ran at night and no matter how good lighting is at the track, you will always need some additional light to look into dark spots.

**Fire Extinguishers.** IKF rules require them, but I never saw one at a race (except mine, of course). IKF

Oil tray, battery/starter unit, battery charger, small parts tray, fire extinguisher. Incidentally, place your number on your starter. It will make it more easily identifiable at the start-finish.

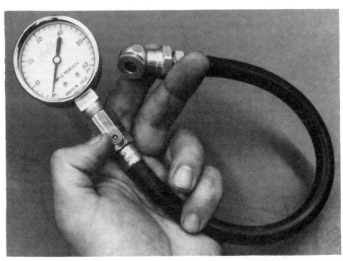

Investing in a good tire gauge is well worth it. This one has a pressure release valve, an easily read dial, a convenient swivel nozzle and a high-grade hose.

Some guys use a little wagon to carry their starter and battery on. OK, but a bit cumbersome.

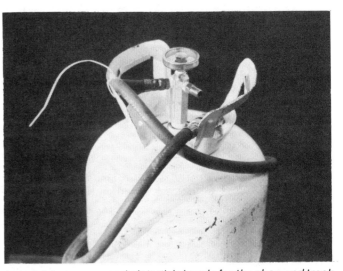

A portable compressed air tank is handy for the shop and track if you can't afford a compressor.

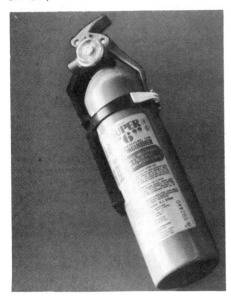

A good fire extinguisher is a good idea to have even if you don't race. IKF and WKA require them in the pits. Use Halon-filled extinguishers. CO² is not legal with some ruling bodies.

rules do not allow CO² extinguishers. A Halon-filled unit is preferred. Extinguishers are a good idea to have even if you don't race.

**Engine Compression Gauge.** Any quality gauge will do. Get the hand-held kind. The ones you screw into the plug hole are nicer, but not necessary.

**Tape Measure.** You'll need one to check stagger (I'll explain what that is later) and to set the front-end alignment. Preferably, get the narrow metal type. A six-footer will do just fine. The cloth-type measures used in sewing will be nice to check stagger.

**Stop Watch.** A stop watch is not absolutely necessary at this point. However, if you have someone take your lap times during your first few events, you will get a real ego charge when you see your lap times drop in later events. Buy a digital watch and be sure it can time at least two laps at a time. Good watches, these days, cost around forty dollars. They can be purchased from most kart shops.

**Parts Tray.** I got one at Safeway in the household department for $1.98. Those trays are just plastic boxes with compartments you can use to separate fasteners and things when you are working on your kart. The trays are especially handy when working on your kart at a night race. Silverware trays will work just as well.

**Oil Trays.** Also required by the IKF and nice to have at home when maintaining your clutch. These trays are metal or plastic, about 3/4-inch high by 16 inches by four inches. The trays are used under the chain and clutch to keep the pits and your garage floor clean. The trays come in very handy when disassembling the clutch.

**Safety Wire.** Not essential to have, but nice when you need it. Expensive to buy, but the stuff will last forever. Unless you have a lot of fasteners to safety wire, you could use mechanic's wire at a fraction of the cost — .032-inch diameter is just right. I like to use safety wire through the exhaust springs. If a spring breaks during a race it will not fall on the track and cause a hazard to other competitors. The safety wire will also keep the exhaust system from falling off altogether.

**Starter/Battery Package.** I prefer the compact model. There are several other models to choose from. Some require a car battery, a stand or wagon to carry all the gear on.

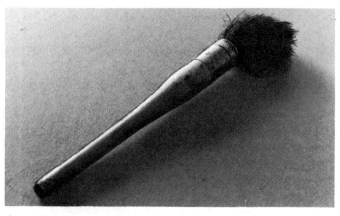

Two different sizes of tie wraps. These are handy to hold wires and hoses in place. The larger ones can be used around frame tubes and to hold number plates on.

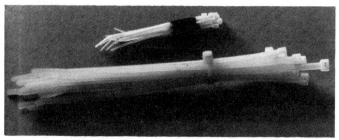

A mechanic's brush is handy to clean around the chain area and in hard-to-reach places.

**Battery Charger.** Get a small charger at your kart shop. Look closely at the amp-hour rate and read instructions on the battery to be sure the two are compatible. The battery should be charged overnight before the race.

**Duct Tape.** Always handy — get a roll or two, preferably from a sheet metal shop. There you will get the real stuff at probably a better price than at the parts store.

**Electrical Tape.** One roll will do and will last you a long time.

**Tie Wraps.** These are narrow plastic strips you wrap around wires, hoses, number plates, etc. They are real handy and don't cost much. Get the thin narrow ones for wires and the broader longer ones for number plates.

**Clipboard and Paper.** You will use the clipboard and paper to take notes. You will make lists at the track — of repairs and modifications needed and parts that you will need to purchase. Also you will need the clipboard to hold your race log sheet and your pre-race checklist. It will help your crew person write down your lap times on your race log sheet.

**Rule Book.** Get one. Being legal in your first few races will not be very critical. However, as you progress I recommend you follow the rules to the letter (and the intent). It is not fun to win knowing you are cheating. It's even less fun to win, being "torn down" and learn your engine, carburetor or fuel is not legal. That is also embarassing. So get a rule book and study it. Again your local kart shop should have a copy or write directly to the sanctioning organizations. Also check "local rules." Each club has its own rules and weight limits.

## You'll Need Chemicals

This area encompasses: lubricants, paints, oils, grease, solvents, brake fluid, clutch oil, air filter spray, hand cleaner, Loctite, silicone gel, and a turkey baster to fill your chain oiler.

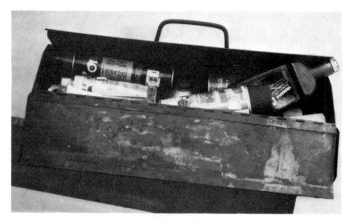

This old Army surplus toolbox made a nice carrying case for lubricants.

You will also need a couple cans of cheap 30- or 40-weight motor oil for your chain oiler (although some guys just use the oil they drained out of their car), and a can of spray for the air filter (again, ask what oil to use with your particular filter). And, if you are running a wet clutch, get a quart of clutch oil.

**Two Cycle Oil.** For two cycle engines, use the oil recommended by the engine manufacturer. Mix according to the engine builder's ratio, not the oil manufacturer's claims.

**Hand Tools.** Dikes, needle-nose pliers, regular pliers, half-round file, rat tail file, 16-inch wood ruler, ball peen hammer, hack saw blades and saw, feeler gauges, socket set, one short and one long extension, open - box end wrenches, small and large crescent wrenches, screwdriver set, small tape measure and a chain breaker.

## Spares You Will Need

**A Chain.** You might as well get a whole length if you can get a good deal. Replace the chain every time it breaks or comes off. If you are going to run several length tracks, I would suggest you use different length chains for different size sprockets. The reason is that if you run a short chain with a large rear gear, the tire will probably rub against the clutch, even if there is a gap between the tire and the clutch when the kart is just setting. You may also run out of adjustment on the frame rails if the chain is too long.

**Gears.** Not absolutely necessary right now, but you will eventually need some of varied sizes for different tracks and track conditions. Do not get the whole range of gears to start, but get maybe every other size. One tooth difference will not make much difference when you are just starting out. Hopefully you got some spares with the kart you bought. Find out the size gear your class runs at the track you intend to run. In sprints and speedway, you will probably run one to four more teeth (driven gear) for at least your first time out.

**Ballast.** Know roughly what you and your kart weigh without fuel. If you are over the weight limit, consider running a higher weight class. If you are under the weight, you should consider a lower weight class. If you find yourself way above the weight of the higher weight class, you need to go on a diet and lose some weight. In any case, if you are under the limit of the class you are going to regularly run, you will need to get some ballast. Buy some lead from a scrap metal dealer and **bolt** the weight onto the frame with safety lock nuts, cotter pins and/or safety wire. Repeat, **bolt** it on. Ballast will not stay with hose clamps, wire, or tie wraps. Not only is it unsafe not to bolt on your lead, but if you lose it you will certainly be disqualified when you get on the scale after the race. Someone could also be hit by the weight flying off.

**Stand.** Hopefully you got one with your kart. If you are handy, you can make one out of square tubing and a small chain. Saw horses will get you by for a while if you are tight on bucks.

These deburring tools are very handy. They can be used to deburr holes and sharp edges. A smooth edge relieves stress and prevents cut knuckles.

Kart stands are nice at the track but saw horses can also be used. Their advantage is that you can load and unload the kart by yourself.

Exhaust flex and spare gears. That's close to $300 setting there.

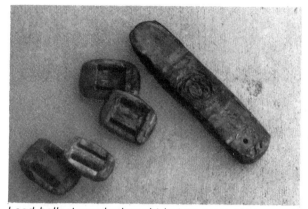

*Lead ballast can be bought in two-pound increments from skin diving shops. Scrap metal places will be much less expensive, however, the selection will be rather limited*

## Clothing

**Helmet.** Be sure that the helmet you are buying is "SNELL"-approved. The Snell Foundation was named in the memory of the race driver of the same name who died of injuries received in a race car accident. The Snell Foundation only tests and approves protective headgear. A helmet not Snell-approved does not mean it is unsafe. Some polycarbonate helmets are said to be just as good, if not better, than the fiberglass approved helmets. However, the Snell Foundation does not own the equipment necessary to test polycarbonate helmets and since the Foundation is non-profit, it cannot, at this time, test some newer material helmets. Your second consideration is availability of face shields. The Moto 3 by Bell, for example, does not come with a shield. That helmet is OK for motocross, but it will not take tear offs. If you get a helmet that does not have face shields made for it, you will have to wear goggles or you will have to have face shields custom made. Also be sure the shield comes with metal snap buttons for the tear offs. In choosing a helmet, be certain it is not too tight or too loose. Your head will swell some on a hot day and the padding on the inside will compress after you have worn the gear a few times. The chin strap should be good and tight. Too tight is better than too loose. Remember that the helmet will settle down on your head with bumps and vibrations. Do not skimp on your helmet. Some years ago Bell helmets ran a slogan that read, "If you have a ten-dollar head, buy a ten-dollar helmet." Just get a Snell-approved helmet and you will be fine. The helmet should also bear the latest Snell sticker. Check the latest rules and see to it that your helmet complies.

**Tear Offs.** Tear offs are clear plastic strips you drape over your face shield. When your shield gets muddy, you just reach the end of the tear off and pull it off. Guys stack as many as ten tear offs at a time when racing in mud. You may need one or two on asphalt. See the picture to learn how to stack up your tear offs the right way.

**Gloves.** Motocross gloves will give you maximum protection in case of a crash. Good gloves will also protect you against mud clods and keep your fingers from getting burnt

if you change the carburetor setting during the race. Gloves will also come in handy should you need to work on the exhaust system in between rounds.

**Shoes.** Most guys just wear old tennies. Those feel fine to drive in, but safety-wise I would prefer a low boot.

**Leathers.** Leathers are ideal for any form of karting. Unfortunately, the cost of leathers is rather high. However, in a crash, the driver is inevitably thrown out of the kart. The odds of making a soft landing are pretty slim and the poor driver will often skid on his body for several yards. This can be very painful, even wearing leathers. Leathers are nice because they will not tear or puncture when the driver is sliding on the ground. The second best choice is a one-piece driving suit. Ideally get a one-piece suit, because the jacket will not roll up on you and leave nasty scratches on your torso. A driving suit is not an essential item. I'd rather see you spend your hard-earned dollars on more important things. However, if you can afford one, go for it. A nice suit really improves your image and does improve your attitude, but do avoid the "cool look syndrome." You are better winning a race in old Levis and spend your money on good tires rather than finishing in the middle of the pack with a new suit on. Remember that looking cool is nothing and winning is everything. Basically, a pair of strong Levis with a good belt, a T shirt and heavy jacket will do. Be sure the jacket does not come unzipped with the air speed as it could get tangled in a wheel or the chain. Enduros require leathers for their races.

*A fully dressed driver looks like something out of "Star Wars." The elbow pad protects the arm against bruises by banging on the engine. Note heavy weight lifting belt.*

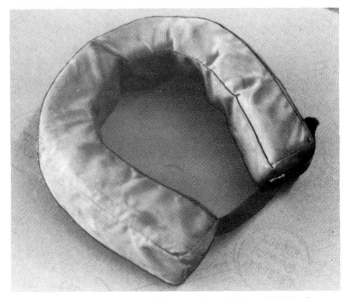

Neck braces are now mandatory by the IKF and WKA. Get one even if you run an outlaw track.

This mild-mannered transporter can be transformed into a Yamahauler in minutes. And yes, the driver can still get in this car. I do not recommend using such a small car. I ended up tearing the headliner and the carpet.

**Neck Collars.** These are only necessary if you crash. Since you never know when you are going to crash . . . get one. They are around thirty dollars and if you flip, one may literally save your neck. Neck collars are required by the IKF for 1984.

**Leather Belts.** A heavy-duty weight lifting belt will give your back support and help prevent injuries in case of a crash. A good belt will also help prevent "morning after" backaches and will help take up the nastier bumps in the track. Those belts are available from K&P Manufacturing in Azusa, CA.

**Tow Car.** This is probably one of those "bring what you have"-type things. I have a Pinto hatchback that I jam full of stuff once a week (and I mean jam) and it serves its purpose. If you are tight on money, whatever will get you there is fine. If you can afford it, a van or pickup is ideal. For a pickup, get a shell so you can lock up your belongings. Again, looking cool is not important — getting there (first) is.

All your gear will fit in one of those bags. They are cheap and very handy.

# 4
# Handling And Kart Set-Up

This chapter is not going to be an esoteric essay on the engineering dynamics of tire adhesion, aerodynamics and lateral "G" forces. This subject will be expanded on later in another book for more advanced racers. Of any part in motor racing, steering, suspension and handling in general are the most misunderstood and misused elements (and, yes, karts have a form of suspension system in the frame and tires).

You can't really go wrong building a stock car frame, or even the engine, if you follow some general guidelines and you used off-the-shelf items that were race-proven such as cams, rods, pistons, heads, etc. Suspension and handling are much more complex. A kart has no springs, swing arms, shocks or sway bars to complicate things. Springs allow weight to shift in corners, which in turn changes swing arm and rear axle angles. This movement then changes wheel and tie rod angles. However, a kart, without a suspension, is complicated by its own simplicity. We have very few adjustments that can be done on a kart. Some adjustments make minute changes in the handling and responsiveness of the machine. A kart, like any other motor vehicle, is an extension of the driver's brain. The racing machine (whether a kart, a boat, a motocross bike or an Indy car) will only do what the driver makes it do. The machine cannot do what the driver wants it to do if the machine is not set up properly. Certainly a driver can induce a certain attitude in a racing vehicle, but it will be at the expense of lap times and/or safety. On the other side of the coin, a certain handling

characteristic can be overcome with a particular driving technique, which could be detrimental (or non-maximizing) to lap times. "Make up" driving techniques are often dangerous.

Handling can best be described as "how a vehicle responds to driver input under a certain condition." For example, a car would round a turn at its maximum speed without losing any time whatsoever. This would be called excellent handling, even though the car had to round the turn completely sideways, because our example is a sprint car with unlimited power. Let's now take a speedway kart with 10 or 15 horsepower and 350 pounds of driver, kart, fuel and ballast. The same handling characteristic would be totally detrimental, due to the amount of tire scrub wasting the low-power output of the motor.

Handling should be tailored to:
— The type of vehicle being raced
— The type of surface being raced on (asphalt, dirt, ice)
— The amount of power available to the driver
— Safety
— Driving style (although I feel there is only one way to drive a vehicle around a track at maximum speed)
— Gearing
— Tires
— Driver's experience
— Weather
— Length of race
The goal for any motor racing vehicle, is to achieve

*"Proline" front end. Note tubular tie rods.*

*Here is a nifty way to fasten the bumper. The nut at the end will prevent damage to the threads while loading the kart on the scales. The jam nut will allow the bolt to be held for easy removal.*

maximum cornering force. This force is also called "lateral acceleration" and is measured in "G" forces ("G" stands for gravitational).

The only way to get maximum lateral acceleration is to utilize the tire contact patches to their maximum. There are several inputs and phenomena that influence handling and lateral acceleration, but everything boils down to the bottom line (literally) —— the tire contact patch. If we want to achieve maximum cornering force we must fulfill the following requirements: 1) The front and rear tires are heated evenly (fronts are the same and rears are the same), 2) Tires are the largest available, 3) The tires are working at their optimum temperatures and 4) Tire temperatures are even across their surface. Only then do we achieve the maximum lateral acceleration possible. It's that simple, but then again, it's not. Most race tracks have more than one turn. The handling must be set up for all the turns. This is obviously impossible, so at best we must reach the optimum compromise — the compromise giving the fastest lap times.

Let's take a look at an example of compromise: We are racing at the Indianapolis Motor Speedway. The track is used, with all four turns, exactly the way it is used for the "500." However, in the middle of the front straight we have an "S"-shaped chicane that must be taken at about 30 MPH. Naturally, you would set up to take the four fastest turns as fast as possible and you would have to live with whatever this set up would bring in the "S" turn. You may lose a few miles per hour for a few feet on the track, but you will make that up tenfold in the faster corners and you will carry that speed for almost 2.5 miles.

Let's look at the many factors influencing go kart handling. The first and most important is tire loading. The more load is placed on a tire the more (within reason) traction a tire will have. The best example is the kart turning on two wheels. The inside wheels have absolutely no traction. A kart, set up properly, will turn with an equal amount of weight on the front and the rear wheels respectively. Based on this you can see how critical weight transfer is. Adding weight is detrimental to overall speed because the added weight must be accelerated forward, backward and sideways. Shifting weight is the correct method. Ballast can be positioned in the light areas, but most importantly, the driver's weight can be positioned, via the seat, in such a way as to provide the weight distribution we are looking for. The driver's weight is the largest movable mass on a kart. The driver's weight can be moved around via the seat. Unfortunately the fiberglass seats currently available do not lend themselves very well to quick repositioning.

Tire loading on karts offers another problem. There is not enough weight available on a kart to load the tires effectively. Common practice on stock cars and open wheel circle track cars is to run more weight on the inside to minimize unloading of the left tires while turning. This method can be used on speedway karts, but due to the current tire design and the sizes available, maximized tire loading can be achieved on karts by running a relatively high center of gravity and using as small a tire as possible without affecting overall speed and safety.

Preparing a car or a kart for action should always start on a surface plate or scales. Surface plates are very expensive to build and are used mainly for stock cars. Scales are much less expensive and are ideal for karts. Four bathroom scales will work perfectly for karting. One scale can also be used effectively, but this is more time consuming. If you use less than four scales, the wheels not being weighed must be supported by blocks the same thickness as the scales to provide even support on all four corners. The tire contact patches must completely cover the scale surface or the blocks. This will ensure that any camber at the front, and tire bulge, will rest on the weighing surface. Note all four corner weights without the driver in the kart and with the ballast removed. Front tire circumference should be equal and rear tires should also be of same circumferences. If you have different tires on any of the corners, change the pressures until you have zero stagger front and rear. If your machine has adjustable spindles, set them evenly in height and use the same number of shims on both sides for the offset. Also set rear wheel offset evenly.

Both front wheels should weigh the same, plus or minus two to four pounds. If one side weighs differently than the other, the frame is bent. See the section on frame straight-

Set go-kart on perfectly level surface. This plate was built and then shimmed to level. A level floor will do. You can also use floor tile squares under the tires to bring the frame to level.

Scale should also come in complete contact with the tire contact patch. Set scale in same position for all wheels. Record front end weights and compare. A difference of two or three pounds generally indicates a bent frame. Be sure tires are the same circumferences, spindles are at the same heights and camber is set at near zero on both front wheels.

A block the same thickness as the scale must be used on opposite wheel of same end if you are only using one scale. This particular block is too narrow. The block should cover the entire tire contact patch, so as to be in contact with the lowest portion of the tire. Camber angle and/or bulge will influence the readings. Bring stagger to even and set camber to zero. Then weigh the kart again with the camber back to where you want it and note the weights for future reference.

Use this method if left front shows more weight. If the right side is too heavy, reverse the set-up. A person could stand or sit on the rear tire, but the car bumper makes this a one-man job.

Kart #6 is sideways wasting power and time, while #7 is putting power to the ground and passing #6. Note right front tire on #7. The tire is working and getting traction. Note the left front wheel of #6 is off the ground and at incorrect camber angle. This chassis is obviously too soft and is causing excessive right rear weight transfer.

*This tool is used to check corner weights. Scales are more accurate for checking frame straightness.*

enduros, the weight on each side must be equal, unless you are racing on an oval track or on a track with more important turns on one side than the other. Front-to-rear ratios should be closer to 41/59, driver on board.

While on the scales, play with tire stagger, ballast distribution, driver seating positions and spindle heights. Note those figures and keep them as permanent records. If you have a handling problem later on, you will have some data to fall back on to make corrections.

Here is the key to using your scale data: If the kart pushes (understeers), add weight to the front. If the car is loose (oversteers), increase rear weight. The scales will tell you exactly how much weight to shift around. Weight distribution will get you close to maximum handling performance. You may still need to shift some weight around after you make a few laps. After weight distribution is balanced, you may want to fine-tune your chassis with spindle heights. Refer to the handling chart to determine proper changes. Again, if the frame is straight and the weight distribution is correct, you should not have to fool with spindle heights, front stagger, alignment, Ackerman, etc.

ening in this book and go back to the scales until the correct weights are reached.

Never bend your frame to try to cure a handling problem. The frame is your starting point. Like the foundation of a house, it is a base to build on. If you start a fraction off and build on the error, you will end up off a double digit. I cannot stress this enough! Bending the frame will not only add insult to injury, but repeated bending will weaken the metal and you will end up with a noodle for a go kart. Keep frame straightening for the times your kart needs "depretzelizing." Bending a frame to make up for a handling problem will never give you maximum cornering force because the original problem that prompted you to bend the chassis in the first place is still there — you are only covering up the problem, not solving it. Look at it this way: If your family car has a low front tire, would you reduce the pressure in the other tire? Of course not. You would add air to the low tire and that will make the car steer straight again.

You see guys at the track "adjusting" their frame. They will never know precisely what they did and each time they use that method, they weaken their frame a bit more.

In case of a crash, yes, do the best you can at the track so you can finish your race. Go back on the scales before the next event. That's exactly what the pro teams would do.

## Weight Distribution

For speedway you should have 42 to 38 percent weight in the front and 58 to 62 percent on the rear. Try to stay near 60 percent in the rear, but no more than 62. The kart should also have 55 to 60 percent of the total weight on the inside two wheels. Use the regular driver, with helmet on when weighing the kart. For sprints and

## Oversteer and Understeer

Oversteer is synonymous to loose, and understeer is the same as pushing. Pushing and loose are terms used by the dirt boys while oversteer and understeer are used by the guys with clean fingernails. Understeer is the phenomenon experienced when cornering a car (or kart) whose front tires have reached their limit of adhesion before the rear tires. Oversteer occurs when the rear tires lose traction first. If you have ever seen a sprint car or speedway bike in action, you will immediately recognize oversteer.

For a speedway kart you should try to achieve a neutral attitude. The reason is that a tire sliding sideways eats up a

*Notice extreme camber change on the left front wheel of this kart. This is undesirable because only the inside part of the tire is in contact with the track, thus losing considerable traction.*

*Another nice innovation by Emmick. Quick adjustable spindles for the dirt. These could also be used in sprints to balance out the frame should it flex.*

lot of power. The tire is wasting those precious ponies you spent all those precious dollars on. A sprint car can derive more speed by being sideways for two reasons. One, the driver has ample power at his disposal, and two, a sprint car suspension is designed to transfer weight to the ground where the power can be converted to forward motion. Now, take a kart weighing 350 pounds with driver and fuel. At 15 horsepower, that's about 23 pounds per horsepower. A sprint car weighs around 1300 pounds, but it also puts out some 600 horsepower. That's 2.1 pounds per horsepower, or almost ten times more than a kart.

Remember that a kart uses a straight axle in the rear. Both rear wheels are always trying to turn at the same speed. The problem with that is that in a turn the inside wheel should be turning more slowly than the outside wheel. Thus one of the rear wheels will be slipping by a certain amount and scrubbing off speed. That's at best. Now if you hang the rear end out, both rear wheels will be scrubbing speed and losing traction and forward acceleration. Conserve that power as if it were gold. With a kart you have very limited amounts of power to play with. If you waste say, one and a half horsepower, that is 10 percent of your total power supply. Ask any of the guys at the track what they would pay for a 10 percent increase in power. Instead of looking for new horses, use the ones you already have judiciously and get every drop of power on the ground. What was just discussed is added proof that it does not take "megabucks" to be competitive in karting. Just do not waste the power you already have, and let the other racers spend their money on tricked-out motors and watch their money go up in rooster tails on the dirt or smoke on asphalt.

## Factors Influencing Handling

Again, I do not want to get too involved in the area of

steering, handling and suspension theory. We have included a handy chart to help you overcome basic handling ills. If you have set your weight distribution properly, and you use the handling chart correctly, you will be years ahead of other beginners (and many more experienced racers).

## Toe In, Toe Out, Alignment

The way the front wheels are pointed toward the front is commonly called wheel alignment. A smaller distance between the forward facing surfaces of the tires as compared to the rear facing surfaces is called "toe-in." The opposite is called "toe-out."

A small amount of toe-in helps the vehicle steer straight, without darting from side to side. Some toe-in also allows a smooth transition from a straight line to a turn position. Toe-out will cause darting down the straights and corner entry oversteer. Toe-out will also cause a nasty, violent transition from a straight line to the turning position. Use from 0 to 1/8-inch of toe-in.

Measure the distance between the front and the rear of the front tires at the center line of the tire. In other words, draw an imaginary horizontal line across the center of the wheel bearings and take your measurements where this line crosses the front and rear of your front tires. Check this setting before each race.

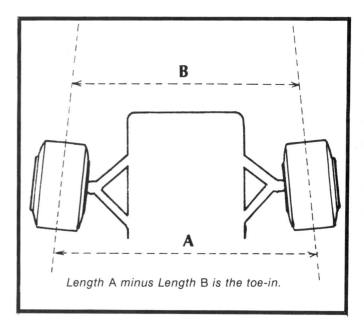

*Length A minus Length B is the toe-in.*

## Camber

Camber is the wheel and tire inclination at the top. Camber is measured in degrees and fractions of a degree. When the top of the wheel is inclined toward the middle of the car you have negative camber. If the top of the wheels are pointing out, it is positive camber. Optimum camber for maximum tire adhesion is 0 to negative 1 degree. Negative 1/2-degree is best. These figures are dynamic, meaning the

(Below) This wheel alignment tool is available from GEM Products. It is simply a collapsible shaft with a set screw to hold the measurement in position. Set the width to correspond to the distance between the two lines you have drawn. Draw an imaginary line through the center of the tire from front to rear and draw a mark on the tire where this new line intersects the first line you scribed. Do this both front and rear and use the intersection points to take the measurements from. First take a measurement from the rear of the tires, lock the alignment tool and move to the front of the tires. Align one end of the tool with one of the marks and look at the other end of the rod. If the line is to the outside of the end of the rod, you have toe-out. If the line is on the inside of the rod, you have toe-in. Adjust the tie rods to give you the desired amount of toe.

(Above) First use a screwdriver to trace a line on the front tires. Secure hand and screwdriver against a solid base to get a good straight line all the way around the tires. You now have a reference point to measure from.

There's an easier way, too. The front end alignment can be set easily with a tape measure. Be certain the measurements are taken directly across the bearing centerline.

figure is taken with the wheels turned. The reason for doing this is that, depending on front end geometry, the camber will change as the front wheels are turned. On an oval track you would want to dial in some negative camber in the right front and some positive in the left front. The left front wheel will end up with 0 to positive 1 degree of camber. If you turn right and left, negative 1/2 degree will be optimum on both sides. The static setting (wheels straight) means nothing and should only be used as a reference point.

If you turn in both directions and the insides of the tires are scuffed more than the outside, you need more positive camber. If you turn only left and the inside of the right tire is scuffed more than the outside, and the outside of your left front shows the wear, you need more positive camber in the right and more negative on the left. This problem would show up immediately if you use a tire pyrometer. Rear wheels of a kart have no camber because both rear wheels run off the same straight axle.

*Typical example of excessive negative camber. This problem can be solved by adding some positive camber and reducing caster. In this case only two-thirds of the tire is on the ground.*

## Caster

Caster can best be described as steering lead. Look at the front forks of a bicycle. Note how the forks lead forward at the wheel as compared to the mounting point at the handle bars. Spindles in karts (and all other wheeled vehicles) are mounted in such a way. If the top of the spindle is inclined rearward you have positive caster. If the spindle top is inclined forward you have negative caster. Negative caster is no longer used because it causes straight line instability. Positive caster centers the front wheels and assists in making th vehicle steer straight without wandering. Caster will change the camber in a front end as the front wheels are turned. Turn the front wheels of a bicycle or a motorcycle and you will have the best visual explanation of caster you can ask for.

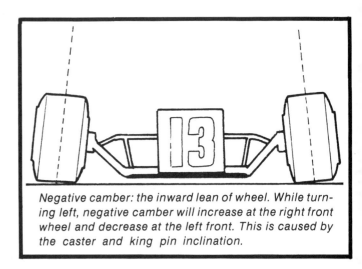

*Negative camber: the inward lean of wheel. While turning left, negative camber will increase at the right front wheel and decrease at the left front. This is caused by the caster and king pin inclination.*

## Kingpin Inclination

Kingpin inclination is the angle one could see from the front or the rear of the vehicle. K.I. is always top inward. Kingpin inclination is used to assist caster in centering steering and it reduces force to turn the steering wheel. K.I. changes camber as wheels are turned. Since kingpin inclination and caster negate each other's effect on camber, you should try to run just enough caster and kingpin inclination to maintain the desired amount of dynamic camber.

K.I. and caster are generally built into the frame design of a go kart and cannot be changed very easily. The alternative is to have custom spindles built to overcome the amount of camber discrepancy. This will prove to be rather expensive since it is going to be a trial and error situation. Remember that the camber goes positive on the left wheel, as you turn left, proportionately to the right which goes negative.

## Ackerman Steering Effect

As a car or kart goes around a corner the right side wheels are forming a different radius than the left side wheels. Picture this: A car 20 feet wide going around a turn.

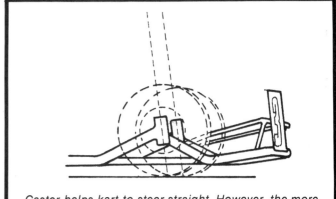

*Caster helps kart to steer straight. However, the more the caster is increased, the more steering effort is required. Caster also causes camber change in turns.*

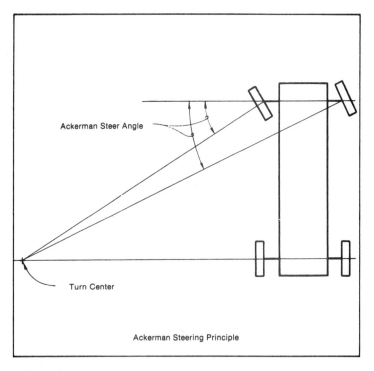

Ackerman Steering Principle

*This driver is correcting the oversteer slide by shifting his weight to the left.*

This example is grossly exaggerated but it will clearly show that the inside wheels turn at a tighter radius than the outside wheels. A German engineer — Ackerman — realized this difficulty in the days of horse and buggy transportation and designed geometry into the steering mechanisms of those days. This geometry is built into your kart front end, cars, buses, trucks, even snowmobiles. There is only one setting that will make both front wheels work together. Add more Ackerman and the inside front wheel will turn too much and scrub off speed, too little Ackerman and the inside front wheel will not turn enough and will cause a toe-in situation, also causing loss of traction. Do not listen to those guys who tell you to crank in more Ackerman for the dirt. One last point: Ackerman is less important on long sweepers and the dirt than on tight tracks and asphalt.

## Body Weight

I want you to try this little exercise next time you are out practicing, (not during a race!). Purposely throw your kart sideways. Now move your shoulders back over the axle by applying pressure against the steering wheel and arching your back rearward. This will shift your upper body weight over the rear more. Note what happens — the slide corrects itself! Keep practicing that little gymnastics — knowing instinctively what to do when your kart gets out of shape may some day save you a spin. That exercise will also make you realize the importance of weight distribution. If your kart is set up loose to start with, you can compensate with your body weight by pushing it back over the rear. However, this shoud only be a temporary measure. Adjust your seat as soon as possible and make a note of the way the kart handled, and of the new seat position.

## Tire Stagger

Tire stagger, or just stagger, refers to the differences in circumference between the tires at each end of the axle. Stagger is only used in oval track racing. Indy cars and stockers use stagger in the rear tires to facilitate corner entry and to help reduce corner entry understeer. On karts, stagger is used in the rear because both rear wheels run off the same straight axle. Both rear wheels are trying to turn at the same speed while covering a different distance — obviously one of the tires will be scrubbing off speed. The outside tire is trying to turn at a different speed than the inside tire because it is covering a longer distance than the inside tire. If both tires are the same circumference, at least one tire will be losing traction because it is turning too fast or too slow in relationship to the forward speed. By running a larger circumference on the right side tire, we get closer to having both tires rounding the turn without scrubbing any speed. Note I said "closer." In order to get both rear tires to turn at an equal speed around the turns of an 1/8-mile track, you would need almost an inch of stagger in the rear. This would create tremendous instability and tire scrub down the straights. Rear stagger is accomplished several ways: 1) Using different tire pressures, which is OK if you can still use optimum range pressures. Slicks do not have as much of a range as dirt tires do when it comes to pressures. 2) Using two different brands of tires. This may be tricky in trying to get two different brand tires close enough in size to be used together. 3) Using a newer tire on the outside and an older tire on the inside. 4) The best method is when you install new tires; inflate them to a low pressure (say 12 to 14 pounds) and

*These tires are mounted on different size rims. The rim on the left is too narrow and does not provide enough sidewall support. The tire in the center is well supported by the correct width rim. The rim on the right is so wide that the tire cannot seat completely on the rim. Different rim widths can be used to alter stagger.*

measure the circumferences after letting the wheels and tires sit overnight. Note the new measurements on the wheels with a marker for future reference. Use the smaller unit on the left and the larger one on the right. If you need more stagger, inflate the right side to 30 or 40 pounds and let it set overnight. Note new measurements on the wheels for future reference. Use the smaller unit on the left and the larger tire on the right. If you need more stagger yet, inflate right tire to 40 pounds and place it in the hot sun for a few hours. Release the air back down to the normal racing pressures and measure the circumferences again. The difference between the two circumferences is your stagger. Use 1/4 to 3/4 of an inch of stagger. The longer the track, the less stagger you will need. The tighter the track, the more stagger you will need.

If you run more than 1/2-inch of stagger on a dirt track, you will experience some handling instability down the straight when the track is still wet. That's the rear wheels fighting for traction. Remember that both rear wheels are traveling at the same forward speed but are covering different amount of ground each revolution. You will always have one or the other wheel bite or lose traction, by however small an amount. Positive rear stagger can help reduce corner entry understeer, negative stagger (larger tire on the left side) can help reduce corner entry oversteer. In either case, stagger will work best on vehicles with slightly more weight on the inside (if you turn in one direction only).

Some guys use stagger in the front to overcome a handling problem or to induce a certain handling characteristic. I feel this is incorrect. If you have a handling problem, find the source and the cause of the problem. Use your wheel offsets and weight distribution to set up and correct handling. The theory behind this is that having a size difference in the front wheels, the larger wheel will have more weight on it, thus transfering weight to the opposite corner. For example, a larger right front tire and a smaller left front will help overcome oversteer and help reduce understeer. This is the back door method of setting up handling.

What front stagger (or spindle height adjustment) does is reduce adherence of the front tires to increase rear traction — a typical example of cutting your nose to spite your face.

## Wheel Widths and Offsets

Correct wheel width is important to provide the tire sidewall the support needed to prevent the tire surface from caving in or bulging out. A slick is happier with a rim slightly wider than its tire tread width. A dirt tire will work with a slightly wider rim than its tread, but it is better to have a rim about the same size as the tread or even a bit narrower. To be certain you have the right set up, consult the tire manufacturer and your kart shop to learn what rim widths are available.

Rim widths can be made up with several different rim halves. For instance, an 8-inch rim can be made up with a 7-inch inner and a 1-inch outer, or vice versa. A 4-inch inner and a 4-inch outer could also be used, or any other combination, providing the rims are available. Practicality will dictate the rim half sizes.

One might think that offsetting the rim centerline would affect the leverage on the axle or spindle. Not so, unless we change the track by moving the centerline of the tire itself. Moving the rim centerline will only relocate the mounting hub without altering the effective leverage. The

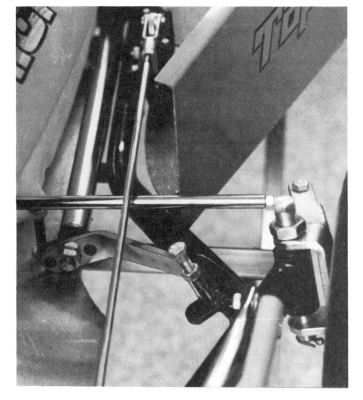

*Weight jack on an Emmick kart. Years ahead of the competition.*

Manufacturers provide ample room for track to move in and out. In this photo, rear wheel is moved all the way in.

This wheel is halfway down the axle. Remember that the further out the rear wheels go, the more bite the front end will have and the looser the rear will be.

All the way out. At this point the kart would be almost impossible to keep on the track. Excessive weight would have to be placed over the rear wheels to create enough bite.

It is a good idea to note amount of axle protrusion on the hub to avoid any confusion.

(Right) Front track adjustment shims on a K&P Supersprint. The further out the front wheels are, the more the rear end will bite. The closer the front wheels are, the more the front end will bite.

centerline of the tires is what determines leverage, in turn altering handling characteristics.

## Tires

Tires have the most important job on any racing vehicle. The tires tie the vehicle to the ground. Everything that is done to improve handling, power, aerodynamics, etc. all end up on the bottom line — the tires. More precisely, the tire contact patch. That little area that could cover the hand of a child, determines whether you will win or lose. Those four little areas determine ulitmately how fast your vehicle will accelerate, brake, corner, and how it will respond to driver input. Needless to say you must pay very close attention to your tires.

Obviously the larger tire contact patch you get on the ground, the more traction you will gain. However, there are a few factors limiting the tire size one can realistically use: 1) Some organizations have limits on tire widths, 2) Availability of rims, 3) Practicality, and 4) Tire availability.

Before you set off for your kart shop with your checkbook to clean out the stock, keep two thoughts in mind: 1) The wider the tire the more vulnerable it is to camber change. This is not a vital factor for the rear end of a kart, but a definite consideration for the front half. 2) The wider a tire, the more traction will be generated, thus more weight transfer and more load on the frame (or springs of a suspended vehicle). This is the reason some karts work

The compound on this tire was too soft for the track conditions. This tire was used on a dry speedway track. A dirt or asphalt slick should have been used for this application.

better than others with a certain tire. The more traction, the stiffer the frame should be.

## Reading Tires

Tires can talk. Actually they write. You must learn to read them. Tires will tell you what your kart is doing, better than the seat of your pants ever will be able to tell you. You can learn to read the tires, or use a tire pyrometer, to record the tire temperatures. On asphalt or hard dirt, a pyrometer is the best method of analyzing the handling via tires. Temperatures tend to be more indicative of the last turn or two. Reading the tires will give a better indication of the situation around the whole track.

Tire temperatures will dictate your front end camber, caster, and kingpin inclination. All the way around, temperatures indicate incorrect tire pressures, and weight distribution — front-to-rear, or in-and-out. Temperatures can also tell you the rubber compound to use.

When it comes to tires, the manufacturer is the best source of information one can ask for. Do not be afraid to ask for his advice, especially if one of their reps is at the event you are attending. That's the best time to pick their brain. Go out of your way to meet the reps, and be sure they remember who you are (a sure-fire way of accomplishing that is to win a few races or set some lap records on their tires). The tire reps appreciate the racer who takes advantage of their knowledge because they know how important tires are to a racing machine. The tire rep will help you win all he can because if you win, his tires also win, and that's the best advertising he can ask for (plus it's free).

Reading tires is an art. An art is learned through years of experience and I do not intend to teach anyone this art with a few words and pictures.

## Tire Pressures

Dirt tires are more forgiving than slicks when it comes to inflation pressures. For dirt tires, use 15 to 20 pounds in the rear and 14 to 18 pounds in the front. With dirt slicks, run 15 to 17 pounds in the rear and 14 to 16 pounds in the front. Whether dirt or asphalt, maintain a maximum of 2 pounds difference between the front and rear tires.

Asphalt slicks vary in pressures, depending on manufacturers and compounds. Again, consult your tire manufacturer for the correct pressures for your application.

## Aerodynamics

For speedway and sprints, forget about aerodynamics. You are wasting your time and money with wings, bodies and "what-have-yous." Wings in speedway and sprints are needless and are just another thing to go wrong. Some guys like to make their karts "look good" with non-functional appendages. Looking cool has nothing to do with racing. To

Wheel weights should be taped on to prevent them from flying off.

The spindle stop bolts should be adjusted to limit the steering lock.

Check starter clearance after installing larger tires, rims or nerf bars. You should try to move the rear wheel on the side of your starter as far out as you think you might someday need it. You do not want to find out your starter shaft is too short when you are sitting on the starting line.

Nice steering shaft support on this "Proline" kart.

me the only thing that's cool is that first place trophy on my fireplace mantle. Some guys go all out and get complete body panels for their karts, because they want to look like Formula 1 car drivers. My attitude toward those guys can be summarized by a spectator's comment after an exhibition race I ran at a speedway motorcycle race. The spectator looked at one of those karts and said, "Is this a big kid's toy or a small man's car?"

If you run enduros, definitely aerodynamics are important. However, this book is not the time and place to get deeply into this subject. Steve Smith Autosports has pub-

lished some very fine books on the subject and I would recommend those publications very highly.

## Handling Problem Reference Checklists

The following checklists show problems which could cause oversteer (first checklist) or understeer (second checklist). These are intended to be an aid in your troubleshooting when a problem exists. Keep in mind that a problem you may experience may be caused by a combination of two or more things. When a number of possibilities exist, make a change of the most apparent one at first. Never make more than one change at a time. After a change has been made, test your kart on the track to determine what effect the change has made (and be sure to keep accurate notes).

## Oversteer Problems

1. Incorrect rear tire pressures and/or rubber compound
2. Front tires too wide in relation to the rears
3. Not enough weight over the rear wheels
4. Excessive weight on left front (speedway)
5. Excessive weight on right rear (speedway)
6. Left front tire circumference too large (speedway)
7. Right front tire circumference too small (speedway)
8. Left front spindle too low in relation to the right spindle (speedway)
9. Driver applying too much throttle (muddy, wet or dry-dusty)
10. Frame bent and/or fatigued, and/or cracked welds
11. Frame too flexible for kart weight, tires, and/or power
12. Front track too narrow in relation to the rear
13. Rear track too wide in relation to the front
14. Incorrect aerodynamics (enduro)
15. Not enough toe-in or too much toe-out.
16. Incorrect rear wheel widths for the tire size
17. Driver overbraking or going in too hard
18. Too much weight over front end
19. Incorrect rear tire compound or tire type.
20. Too much rear stagger (speedway).

## Understeer Problems

1. Incorrect front tire pressures and/or compound
2. Rear tires too wide in relation to the fronts
3. Front tires too narrow in relation to the rears
4. Wrong type of tires (dirts on dry, slicks in wet)
5. Not enough weight on front end
6. Too much weight on rear end
7. Right front tire circumference larger than left (speedway) (Too much right front weight.)
8. Left front tire circumference smaller than right (speedway) (Too much right front weight.)
9. Right front spindle too low in relation to the left (speedway)
10. Left front spindle too high in relation to right (speedway)
11. Too much weight on right front (speedway)
12. Driver going into the turns too fast
13. Frame bent, fatigued or cracked
14. Excessive weight over right front
15. Excessive weight over left rear (speedway)
16. Frame too stiff for weight carried, tires and/or power
17. Front track too wide in relation to the rear
18. Rear track too narrow in relation to the front
19. Too much toe-in
20. Incorrect aerodynamics (enduros)
21. Incorrect Ackerman effect
22. Incorrect dynamic camber
23. Incorrect front wheel widths for tire size
24. Not enough rear stagger (speedway)

## General Handling Problems

Rear end wander while driving down straights in mud or driving over bumps — Caused by excessive rear tire stagger.

Front end darts while driving down straights — Caused by: toe-out or not enough toe-in, bent frame, lack of aerodynamics downforce (enduro), excessive front stagger, excessive spindle height differential.

Front end darts suddenly into turns as soon as wheel is turned — Too much toe-out or not enough toe-in, driver too abrupt in transition phase, excessive aerodynamic downforce (enduros).

Kart loose under power — right spindle not low enough.

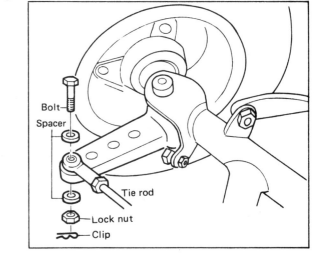

*Typical tie rod end assembly.*          *Courtesy of Yamaha*

### Tire Mounting

*Keep tires in factory wrapping until you need them. Smog, sunlight, heat and cold cause tires to deteriorate.*

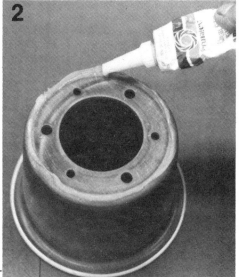

**1**

A tire bead breaker is essential in dismounting kart tires. Breaking the bead by hand is next to impossible and could damage the tire.

The K&P spool wheels compared to the conventional split rim wheels. These rims offer a lower rolling weight, greater strength, and easier tire mounting.

*(Right) Slip rim half, vise grips and O-ring assembly into tire. Line up holes and press down while slipping Allen bolts into their respective holes. Hold two halves together and install washers, lock washers and nuts.*

**2**

To prevent rims from leaking, rub the contacting surfaces on some smooth sandpaper on a flat surface. Also polish the "O" ring seat.
If your rims are old you may have to do this.

Apply a good coat of RTV silicone at the rim edge where the O-ring will seat. Leave rim half flat on the table and slip tire over.

**3**

Slip Allen bolts and washers in rim half with O-ring and valve stem.

**4**

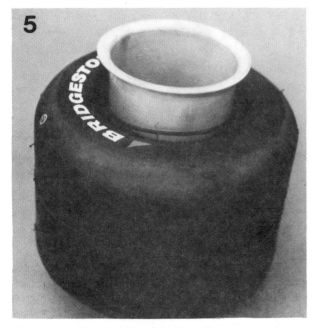

**5**

*Release O-ring and allow it to enter the groove between the two rim halves.*

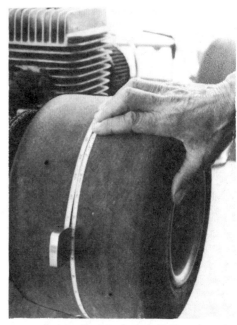

*Wheel need not be mounted on kart before inflating, but the lug bolt pressure will help create a better seal, and being mounted will facilitate measuring stagger. Be sure both tires are inflated to the same pressure. Use around 12 pounds and accurately measure tire circumferences. If you want both tires to be the same size, inflate the smaller tire some more and let it set overnight, then recheck it in the morning after resetting the pressure back to 12 pounds. If you want stagger, take the larger tire and inflate it until you get it stretched out to the desired size. Do not over-inflate as tires or rims may blow.*

*One of the nicest features of the K&P spool wheels is the ease with which tires mount. Use adequate lubrication on the bead and introduce the tire at 45 degrees to the rim. A sharp hit with the palm of the hand will pop the tire right on. The mounting procedure is actually easier with the wheel mounted on the kart.*

**1**

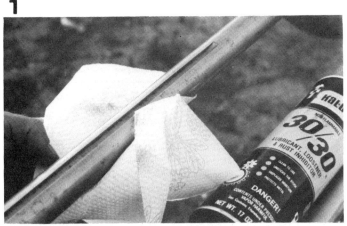

Before installing axle, clean it with a piece of "Scotch Brite" and some lightweight oil or a mineral solvent. Remove any dings with a smooth file and polish lightly with "Scotch Brite" or fine steel wool. Rub axle down with WD40 or 30/30 lubricant which leaves a nice film after drying. Inspect axle as you clean and rub it down with the lubricant.

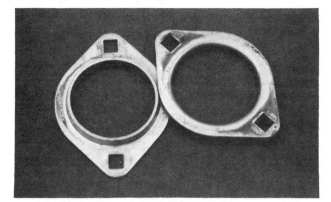

Axle flangettes should be clean and free of dings before installing. A burr in the wrong place could leave the bearing to rotate in the flangettes.

**2**

Install brake hub and disc. On some karts the lock bolt side of the hub might have to go toward the inside of the frame to clear the wheel bearing. You will be able to turn the screw if it is on either side of the hub but the bolt is more easily accessible from the inside of the frame. The key stock should be installed with a spot weld between the bearing and the hub. Should the hub loosen up (which could happen with a lot of heat) the key stock could slip off, leaving the kart without brakes. The spot weld will prevent the key stock from slipping away from the hub. Install bearings and "flangettes." Use grade 5 bolts with lock nuts and washers whenever possible. Leave left side "flangette" loose for now.

**4**

Right side "flangette" should be run on the outside of the hanger, especially if you run speedway. In this position the load is reduced on the bolts, bracket and "flangettes." This also reduces flexing. Do not secure inner bearing locking studs or collars on the axle yet. Tighten right side "flangette" and only snug down the left side. Axle should slip in and out of the bearings freely. If it doesn't, check for burrs or bent axle.

**3**

Measure axle protrusion. Even both sides out and pull the right side out an extra 1/8-inch more than the left. Snug down bearing locking studs or collars to the axle. Do not fully tighten yet. Just snug enough to keep the axle from sliding when you are installing the key stock pieces.

**5**

Cut a piece of key stock long enough to fit snugly between the bearing and the weld at the end of the axle key way. File or grind the end to remove burrs and to square off end. Key stock should slip snugly but easily in the key way. If the key stock shows some resistance it should be inspected along with the key way. Remove burrs or install correct size key stock. Some key stocks are anodized so key will not fit in the slot. Never use force on the key stock as it could crack the axle down the key way.

**6**

**7**

Gently tap the end of the axle until key stock is firmly seated against bearing and weld at end of the axle. Hopefully you do have a weld at the end of your axle. Without the weld the key stock end rests against the snap ring which is not designed to take that kind of load. Repeated pounding will cause snap ring failure and possible los of a wheel and hub. If the axle is allowed to drift on its bearing, it will cause the chain to jump off.

The left "flangette" bolts should be snug. Insert key stock you have cut and filed to fit snugly against weld and bearing. The key stock should be from tight to snug when "flangette" bolts are tightened. Spin axle and see that it spins freely. Tighten bearing set screws or collars. Spin axle again.

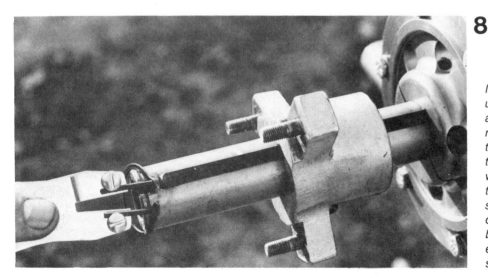

**8**

Install gear and wheel hubs. Leave loose until you have set the chain alignment and the rear tire track. Install the snap rings. A pair of snap ring pliers will make the operation easier and will not distort the rings. If you have the key way welded, the ring is just there to satisfy the tech inspectors. I really feel the weld should be mandatory and the snap ring done away with. Better yet the axle could be ground with a square end at both extremities to provide a solid, square seat to the key stock.

This is an axle bearing collar. Most bearings come with their own set screws. Know what you really need before buying these.

Another style of bearing gear. These collars are a good back up to the bearing set screws.

Flange nuts are nice on wheel lugs. These nuts provide good seating at their base and they do not require washers. Use a "Nylock"-style nut for the lugs and replace them periodically.

Allow plenty of clearance between the tire and the gear. Should the tire hit the gear during cornering the chain will inevitably jump off. The rim should also clear the hub by at least 1/8-inch.

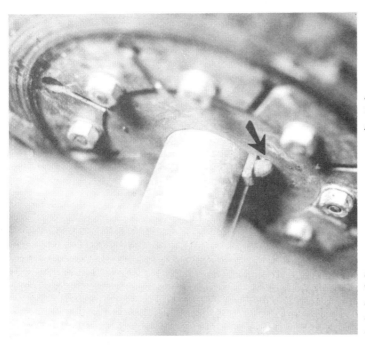

Photo shows weld spot on brake disc hub. This weld spot prevents the key from slipping out from under the hub. Should this happen the rotor would be left free to rotate on axle, leaving the kart without brakes. The weld spot must be between the hub and the bearing.

# 5
# Engines

Yamaha gave karting a super shot in the arm with its new KT series engines. Those motors were designed specifically for karting and have proven very reliable. The KT has taken the spotlight over the venerable McCulloch. The "Mac" was the bread and butter motor of karting for several years. The "KT" has taken over for one simple reason: reliability. The Yamaha will last a whole season without a major rebuild, and possibly more. But you must follow some very basic precautions. If you run another brand of engine, these guidelines will, for the most part, also apply. The first step is to obtain the Yamaha KT 100 book from Steve Smith Autosports or from where you purchased this book. The other maintenance and precautions follow. Most of the information contained in this chapter applies to other two cycles.

*Fuel filters have correct fuel flow direction printed on them. Observe direction or filter will not be as efficient.*

## Accessories

Run a fuel filter. Chances are you will not get any dirt in the gas, but a filter is a good safety measure. Purchase a plastic or metal filter. Glass models tend to break or crack. Most filters have an arrow pointed on their body to indicate fuel flow. Point the arrow toward the carburetor. Use small hose clamps at the filter, fuel tank and carb. Tie wraps do not go on tight enough and may slip off.

## Fuel Line

Use a good quality fuel line. Most kart shops carry "non-hardening" fuel line — use it. Rubber or plain old plastic line

will not last. Plastic hardens and rubber cracks. A cracked or hardened fuel line will give some really strange problems. The carburetor will suck some air, at times, and will cause the engine to miss or stall. A hard fuel line will slip off. The end result of this mishap is obvious.

Replace fuel lines once or twice a year. The fuel system gets more damage from setting than from daily use. Include fuel system inspection in your regular maintenance routine.

## Idle Setting

Set idle speed according to manufacturer's recommendations. Idle should not be set so low that the engine

*(Left) The carburetor pulse line requires some attention. Be sure it is secured properly and that it has not hardened or cracked.*

*A small piece of foam over the carb diaphragm will keep out dirt and moisture while allowing the diaphragm to still breathe. Just above the foam is the throttle fine adjustment.*

could die. Most kart clutch mechanisms do not allow any engine braking. If you lift off the gas to slow down you might get back on the throttle with a dead engine behind it. Follow engine manufacturer's settings and you should be in good shape.

## Throttle Cable Setting

Fine-tune the carburetor butterfly opening with the adjustment at the carb. Your goal is to make the carburetor open fully without putting any strain on the cable. Use a small open end wrench to open and tighten the locknut. A small crescent wrench will work also. I think it is a good idea to install a piece of foam rubber where the nylon sheath meets the carburetor stay. Also install some foam where the cable enters the sheath and brass fittings at the frame (see photo). This precaution may save you a stuck throttle, especially if you run on a sandy speedway track.

## Air Filters

Most people use K&N air filters. Some guys also use a "sock." I found socks tend to make your engine a bit richer, which leads me to think that socks restrict air flow somewhat. Run a sock if the track is very muddy and remove it after the track dries.

K&N filters are probably the most widely used filters in dirt racing. Those filters will give you great service if you treat them right. Follow the instructions outlined in this book on how to clean the K&N air filters. If you run another brand of

*A piece of fuel line mounted at the end of the throttle sheath will keep the nylon tube from popping out of its socket.*

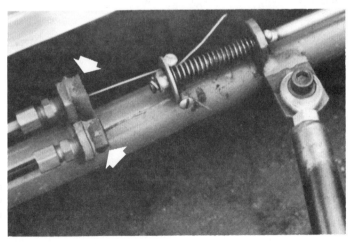

*(Right) Installing little foam strips at the throttle cable orifice will keep dirt out of the cable sheath. Note neat and simple installation of throttle cable and cotter pin at end of throttle rod.*

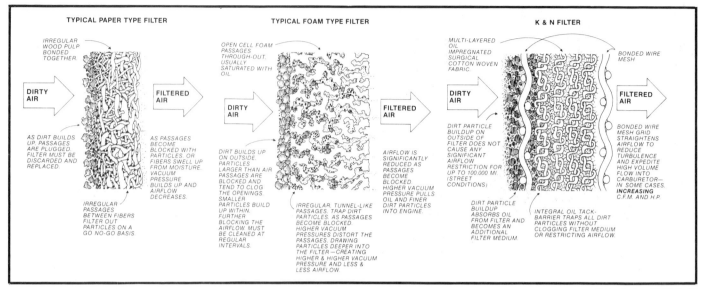

*Courtesy of K & N*

*K&N air filters should be sprayed with K&N's air filter oil before using. Be sure filter has been washed and dried properly before spraying. The K&N spray has the advantage of going on bright red so you can see how much spray you have applied.*

## OPEN STACK EXPOSED TO HIGH SPEED AIRFLOW

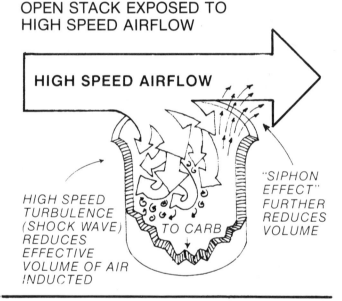

HIGH SPEED AIRFLOW

HIGH SPEED TURBULENCE (SHOCK WAVE) REDUCES EFFECTIVE VOLUME OF AIR INDUCTED

TO CARB

"SIPHON EFFECT" FURTHER REDUCES VOLUME

*Courtesy of K & N*

*This soup bowl over the air filter is basically a good idea, but it restricts airflow somewhat and may cause an overly rich situation at higher speeds. The foam sock over the filter definitely cuts down performance. The bowl is only neccessary if you race on dirt.*

filter, follow manufacturer's recommendations or you may end up with an engine full of dirt. Purchase the spray recommended for your brand of filter. Tighten the clamp snugly at the filter mount. Filters are another one of those things that tend to fall off easily.

## Cleaning Engines

The best method of cleaning is with a sprayer, hot water and Tide. Those sprayers can be bought at lumber yards, hardware stores or discount stores. Tide or most laundry detergents will get the grease off, if you use super hot water. If you go to a quarter car wash, beware of the nozzle pressure against the engine ignition cover. Mositure can enter the ignition cover and remain in the housing. When this happens, the coil will eventually short out and cost you a

Install a rag around your exhaust flex before hosing off kart. This will prevent any water from seeping into the engine through the exhaust passage.

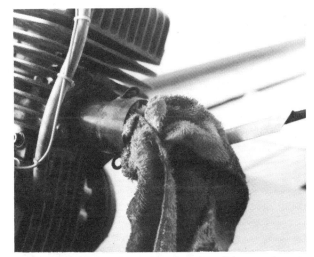

Stuff a rag in the exhaust header when it is open to prevent dirt and foreign objects from falling into the motor.

Drill a hole at the base of the engine electrical cover and install a cotter pin to keep the passageway open. Water can enter the cover and ruin the electricals. The hole will allow moisture to drain out. Be careful when cleaning the kart with a water hose or steam nozzle.

plugs tend to foul too easily. Weather and atmospheric conditions may change the plug heat range required on a particular day. When reinstalling the plug, use caution not to overtighten it, especially if the engine is still warm. Use a little white grease on the threads. If you run a temp gauge, use caution with the sensor under the plug. Replace the plug every four or five races.

race along with several dollars. A good solution is to notch the base of the ignition cover and install a cotter pin in the notch. The pin will move around and prevent the hole from plugging up. Use caution and you should not have any problems.

Another area water tends to creep into is the exhaust flex joint. Wrap a rag around the flex just to be safe. Pressure should also be kept out of wheel bearings and tie rod ends. The pressure pushes water and dirt into the bearings, with obvious consequences.

## Spark Plugs

Reading plugs is an art somewhat like reading tires. It takes time to learn.

If you run a stock Yamaha, use a Nippondenso #N29ESGU. That plug will get you in the right area. Other

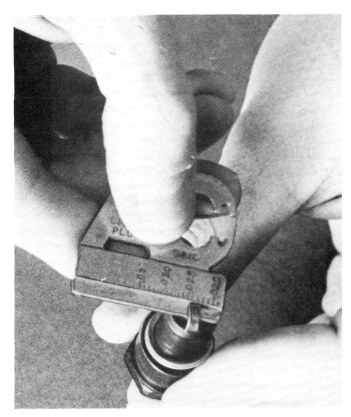

Check that gap to the setting recommended by the plug manufacturer. Auto parts stores sell tapered plug gapping tools that make the job super accurate and fast.

Use special care when installing the spark plug if you run a temperature gauge. Be cautious that the spark plug seats properly into the bottom of the sending unit. You should also remove the plug gasket to insure correct plug tip protrusion into the combustion chamber.

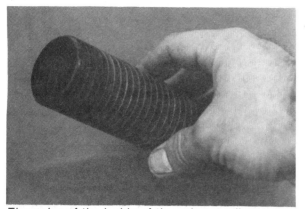

The color of the inside of the exhaust tells a story. Black it is running too rich, white is too lean. Dark gray to chocolate brown is perfect. Remember that unleaded fuel will burn darker than leaded.

## Compression Test

Run a check in between each race. Follow this procedure: Warm up the engine, shut it down and remove the plug. (Never pull the plug cap off to kill the engine. This will result in electrical component failure.) Hold the throttle wide open, insert the gauge into the plug hole and hold it down firmly while you crank the engine over. A good blueprinted Yamaha will put out 115 to 120 pounds of compression. It is a good idea to check the compression after you rebuild your motor so you will have a comparative base to work from. Tear down the top end if you have lost more than five pounds of compression. Inspect the combustion chamber, the piston and cylinder. Take all vital measurements and repair as needed. Hone the cylinder and replace the ring and piston if needed. Follow instructions in the repair manual or have a professional engine builder repair your motor. Check the piston top for color; black to dark brown is acceptable. Grey or white is too lean and you are asking for trouble.

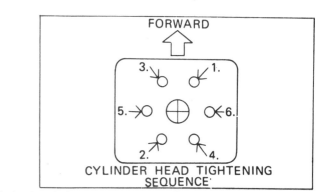

Cylinder head tightening sequence for any engine with six-head studs or bolts. (Courtesy of Yamaha)

## Head and Cylinder Torque

On a Yamaha, torque the cylinder to 225 inch/pounds and head bolts to 175 inch/pounds. The Yamaha book calls for a much higher figure than that, but most engine builders I have spoken to have experienced studs pulling out of the cases. Use a staggered pattern for the torquing procedures. For the cylinder, form an imaginary "X" as you tighten the bolts down. Number the studs in a clockwise fashion. Start with 1, then go to 3, then 2 and 4. Never torque down all at once. Go over each bolt three or four times, increasing the torque gradually and evenly. Use the same procedure for the cylinder head. Use a stagger type pattern there also. See diagram for torque sequence. Clean the nuts and the studs before installation.

## Head Gasket

Replace the head gasket each time you remove the cylinder head. Use caution when purchasing new head gaskets. Get the copper gaskets only — the aluminum gaskets are not as good.

Siamese engines are becoming popular. The two crankshafts are bolted together via an adapter plate.

*When turning over an engine with CDI ignition, the plug wire should be grounded to avoid damage to the electricals. Grounding the plug this way is the easiest method.*

## Fuel Oil Mixture

You must mix oil in the fuel if you run a two-cycle engine. The two-cycle engine has no lubricating system and must rely on the oil in the fuel to receive adequate lubrication for the bearings and cylinder walls. Surprisingly, leaning out the amount of oil in the fuel does not change performance if you run a carburetor with an adjustable needle. The reason is that you can adjust the amount of fuel admitted into the engine. With a fixed orifice carburetor, you would have to change the main jet.

The main and rod bearings are lubricated by bathing in the air/fuel/oil mixture swirling around in the crank case. The mixture is then sucked up into the cylinder where it is compressed and then detonated. A single gear kart puts a heavy load on the engine bearings. When coming off a turn, the engine is heavily loaded and lugging because of the high

gear ratio it is pulling. If the bearings lack lubrication they will definitely fail. A kart or motorcycle with a gear box will not suffer so much. Those motors run at higher RPM with less load on the bearings. So, whatever you do, don't use thin fuel/oil ratios hoping to go faster. You will only fry your motor. Do not listen to claims of cleaner plugs, faster starts, and quicker lap times by using a 50-to-1 synthetic oil.

## Clutch

We have included the Horstman clutch instructions in this book. The Horstman clutch is almost universally used in sprint and speedway karts. This clutch will give you great service if you take care of it properly. The procedures Horstman supplies will give you all the information you need for a rebuild or an adjustment. Use Horstman clutch oil and always maintain the correct level. Incidentally, some of the fluid will leak out from around the center shaft. Leakage will stop as soon as the level gets below the lower part of the shaft.

To fill the clutch, use a turkey baster, a small plastic squirt bottle, or a squirt oil can. Remove the filler plug after placing it at 12 o'clock. Rotate the fill hole open until a small amount of fluid leaks out. Keep the hole open at 3 or 9 o'clock while filling the clutch. When fluid starts leaking out, turn the filler hole back to 12 o'clock and install the plug. Be careful when working on the clutch — the fluid can get extremely hot and can cause very severe burns.

Some words of caution: The Horstman clutch will take care of you if you take care of it. There are two sure ways of burning up a clutch. One is by tearing out of the pits as if something was chasing you. Accelerate slowly until you can feel that the clutch linings have stopped slipping. Two is by keeping the throttle on full bore while the kart is spinning out. Guys do that thinking they will

*This is the "TCI" unit. It should be mounted on rubber and away from heat and vibration.*

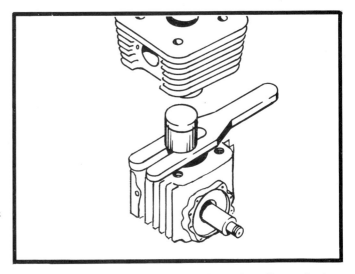

*This tool from GEM is very handy when reinstalling cylinders.*

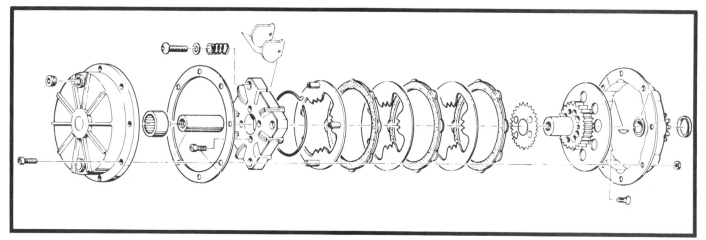

*Horstman disc clutch*

*Courtesy of Horstman Mfg.*

stop and take off faster. All that really does is burn up the clutch linings to a crisp in a hurry.

Next time you have to get into your clutch, install a bolt-on ring (see photo). Those rings will save you a lot of time and aggravation when reinstalling the 8 sockethead bolts. The little nuts on the back of the clutch are sometimes a bit hard to deal with. The ring has tapped holes in it and covers the whole back of the clutch, providing better support to the whole sealing area.

*A warning tag should be used on the clutch to prevent dry running. Running a dry clutch, even for a few minutes, will burn up the lining.*

*This Horstman clutch is equipped with a bolt-on ring. These rings eliminate the use of nuts and provide a more even surface for the gasket to seat on.*

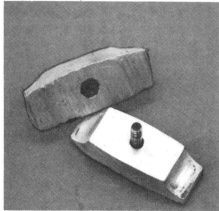

*(Left) These engine mounts are not as accurate as a plate set-up. Keep an eye out for cracks on these mounts.*

*These engine mounting plates are superior to the cast aluminum ones. They are true and allow easier chain adjustment.*

## Chain Guard

A heavy metal guard is imperative. Also get the heavy plastic guards that reach all the way back to the rear bumper (available from Emick Kart Sales). The plastic guard protects the driver from flying chains and oil from the oiler. The metal guards protect the engine from damage by a broken chain. If you run an inboard clutch, install some protective sheet metal on the seat along the chain guard. If the chain breaks, the metal will keep it out of your ribs. Some drivers have been severely injured by broken chains even with an outboard clutch.

## Driving Gear

Take a close look at the clutch driving gear. After some time the teeth wear out to literally nothing. The tip of the teeth will first get razor sharp and after a race or two they will disappear and leave you without power. Take a look at that front gear after every race. Be certain the oiler is working properly and the chain is aligned correctly.

## Clutch Maintenance

Change clutch oil after every race. Remove clutch and inspect after every two racedays.

When clutch is removed, check the following items and replace if necessary:
- Friction discs, if worn below .080" overall thickness (replace)
- Check internal clearance if above .070" and friction discs are still good, then remove the shim.
- Check floaters for warpage.
- Check for broken springs.
- Check for cracks in the drive hub or aluminum weight support.
- Check for wear on the sprocket and bushing on 9T drums.
- Check DXL-23 10-32 x 5/16 flat head screws for tightness, replace every 10 races.
- Install new DXL-20 10-32 x 3/8 cap screws, see below.

NOTE: DXL-20 cap screws are very important, as they hold the drive hub assembly together. Always use new cap screws every time you disassemble the drive hub. Never reuse these screws.

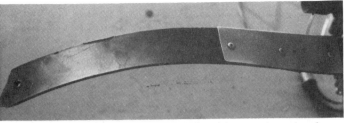

*These long chain guards protect the driver and engine from flying chains and oil.*

*No, the teeth on this gear are not all worn off. This is a gear protector for speedway and sprints. As you can see from the condition of this chain guard, they do work. The drawback is that the guard is so large it will probably hit the track on a bumpy surface and could cause the chain to jump off.*

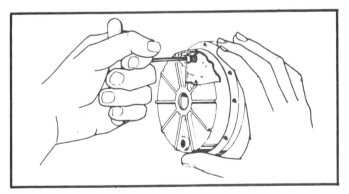

*The clutch will slip more (grab at higher RPM) as the screws are tightened, and it will slip less (grab at lower RPM) when the screws are loosened. Turn the adjustment screws 1/4 turn at a time, then 1/8 turn as the adjustment nears the desired setting. The ideal setting is at the torque peak of the engine which on a Yamaha built to 85 tech rules is around 10,000 RPM, but this figure will vary widely with air density, carb setting, pipe style and flex length.*

*A clutch puller will be needed to break the clutch pack loose from the crank. Never use a hammer on the clutch.*

# 6
# Setting Up For Your First Race

You have read the prior chapters, right? You have your safety equipment, tools, lubricants, a tow vehicle, a fire extinguisher, spares, a stand of some sort, and of course, a go kart. You also checked on rules, class weight engine limitations and you have the tires necessary for the form of racing you are about to participate in. There are a few more things that must be done before you are completely ready for your first race.

## Try Out The Kart

Take your kart to a practice session. There you can lap without any pressure, work out the bugs, and get the feel of racing. A practice session will give you a "dress rehearsal." Some practice sessions have a race at the end of the day, and since there are no points, trophies, or money to be earned, you and the other competitors will not have any pressure on you and it will be a perfect situation to learn. A practice session will give you a chance to set up your handling and experience changing dirt track conditions (if you are running speedway).

Your other alternatives are to take your kart to a vacant lot on a weekend, or if you live in the West, to the desert. Of course, find a safe, smooth surface to practice on. You could set up a small oval track and experiment with different set-ups. Don't get too involved with too much experimentation. Just get the feel of things.

## Flags

Learn the racing flags before you go out to your first event.

**Green:** Race or practice is on. The starter will wave the green flag to start races. Green flag or light will be visible at least at the start-finish line while the track is clear for racing.

**Yellow:** Caution. Hazard on the track. No passing, slow down, use caution. Check local rules on this flag. Some clubs let you race to the yellow, while others make it a yellow condition at the incident only. And, others may enforce a yellow condition all the way around the track. This flag may vary between speedway, sprint or enduro.

**Yellow and Red Waved Together:** Restart. Stop at staging area or start-finish line.

**Red:** Stop. Race has been halted. Go to impound area, or start-finish. No work on the karts allowed.

**White:** One lap left (speedway and sprint).

**White with Red Cross or Spot:** Emergency vehicle on track, use caution.

**Blue:** You are being overtaken by a faster competitor — make room for him.

**Black:** Used against drivers using unsafe tactics. Can also be used for mechanical malfunction. Reduce speed and stop at designated officials' area. A furled black flag can also be pointed at a competitor as a warning. If that driver keeps up whatever he is doing, he will get the black flag next lap around.

**Black and Orange:** Used for mechanical malfunction. Stop immediately at designated area or in your pit area.

**Checkered:** Event is over. Raise hand, slow down and proceed to scales or to your pit area. If the checkered flag is waved in front of you, it does not necessarily mean you have won.

## Kart Prep

**Wheel Offsets.** If you have adjusted the weight distribution as was outlined, you should be close in the handling department. Set the front end evenly in and out on the wheel spacers, and half way up and down on the spindle shims. In the rear, set the wheels 1-1/2-inches from all the way in. For sprints, be sure both rear wheels are equal distance from the frame as the side with the engine is usually limited by the driven gear.

**Gear and Exhaust.** Hopefully you have been able to ask enough knowledgeable people which size gear and length of exhaust flex to run at the track you are going to race on. Install appropriate gear and set the exhaust flex length. I would suggest using 2 to 4 teeth larger (driven gear) than what the more experienced guys are running.

**Ballast.** If you followed the steps we outlined to set up frame and weight distribution you should know the total racing weight of your machine and driver. Install the proper amount of ballast in the correct area to achieve optimum weight distribution. Bring an extra 5 or 10 pounds as some scales vary and you may lose a few pounds by then. Weigh in as soon as possible when you get to the track to allow yourself enough time to adjust the ballast if needed. Weigh in without fuel in the tank and have some weight with you so you can bring the weight up to requirements right then. Ballast must be bolted (and safety wired) safely to the frame. Do not mount ballast to fiberglass or sheet metal. Allow 2 to 4 pounds extra for safety.

*This large PVC tube provides a clever ballast container.*

*Good mounting of ballast. It is mounted on the frame (using an old engine mount) with a good bolt, washers and lock nut. Some organizations may also require safety wire or a cotter pin. Observe the judicious mounting of the wires.*

*This frame is equipped with welded ballast mounts at the steering support bars. Great idea.*

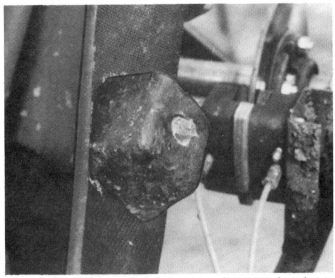

*This lead ballast, mounted on the fiberglass seat, is going to last about as long as a snowball in hell. Fiberglass is not strong enough to support so much weight.*

These two items can be used as mounts for your weights. The block on the left is readily available from most kart shops. The mount on the right is home-made from a seat strut saddle mount with a bolt welded to it.

A vent tube on your gas cap will prevent spillage all over your shiny gas tank. Place a small piece of foam at the end of the tube and you have a dirt-proof system.

An outside sight on the fuel tank is a good idea. Wash out tank thoroughly before doing any welding. Gas tanks will go up like a bomb if they have any fumes left in them while being welded.

"Ratio Rite" and two cycle oil can. The notes on the can save time and possible mistakes.

**Fuel.** Hopefully you are not running an alcohol or exotic fuel class. If you run a four-cycle, use the fuel recommended by engine manufacturer. Leaded premium will provide more octane and some additional lubrication from the lead. For a two-cycle, follow engine manufacturer's or builder's recommendations. use a "Ratio Rite" to mix the oil in the fuel. Again a leaded premium will work best, although two-cycles are not very picky. Unleaded premium is fine. A word of warning: Do not lean out the fuel-to-oil ratio. Leaning out the oil will not improve performance. Not only will reducing the amount of oil in the fuel make no difference in lap times, but if you run a single gear kart you will seize the bottom end of your engine. All it takes is one or perhaps two races. What happens is that with a single gear the engine is heavily loaded coming off the turns and the lack of lubrication will cause the bearings to overheat and eventually seize. Stay away altogether from synthetic 50-to-1 oils. Go with the builder's or manufacturer's advice. Drain the fuel after each event as it may go flat setting in the tank. By the way, fuel/oil mixture runs just fine in your tow vehicle (watch the

Tie a rag on your gas can until oil has been added. It's good insurance. A two cycle motor will self-destruct in a few laps if it is run without oil.

leaded fuel in late model cars though).

**Check Throttle Operation.** Be certain there is no load on the cable when the pedal is fully depressed. See that the carburetor is fully open and returns freely. Hopefully you have installed an extra return spring. If not, do that now!

**Double Check Tires for Leakage.** Don't be concerned if the tires go flat overnight. The tires should be able to hold pressure for a few hours at least. The pressures will be checked before each heat, anyhow.

**Carburetor Setting.** Adjust the carburetor to the manufacturer's or the builder's settings. Remember that turning the needles in will lean out the mixture, and will cause overheating and/or a hole in the piston. If you own a temp gauge, use it. Never let temperature rise over 360 degrees. 325 to 350 degrees is ideal. Usually on a Yamaha you can leave the high speed (short one) set at recommended setting. Use the low speed needle (long one) to adjust mixture, which in turn will alter head temperature. Remember that the higher the elevation of the track, the leaner you can run the carburetor. The reason is that with the higher elevation there is less atmospheric pressure, thus less air is pushed into the carburetor. If you maintain the sea level setting for the carburetor, you will have too much fuel going in the engine in relation to the amount of air taken in. Plugs tend to foul more easily at higher elevations. You may want to run a step hotter plug and have a spare at the start. Only a couple thousand feet of elevation will make a difference. I feel Yamaha recommends too cold a plug for their engines. Especially for a novice, I feel you should try a step hotter plug. Try a 29ESGU at first and see how it runs. The ceramic should be white to light brown. The area around the ceramic should be brown to gray. The ceramic indicates heat range and the area around the outside of the ceramic shows the fuel mixture. You can also get a good idea of how the engine

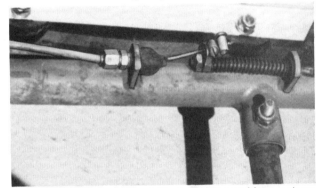

If you run speedway, you should install a piece of foam where the throttle cable enters its frame fitting. The foam will keep dirt out of the housing and prevent a stuck throttle. Note simple method of fastening throttle cable to rod. Here you can also see how much larger the butt tube is which is welded on the frame, compared to the nerf that goes into it. The added room allows the frame to twist without being bound by the nerfs.

An extra throttle return spring is a good idea. Avoid anchoring the spring to the seat because the tension will vary as the engine is moved for chain adjustment.

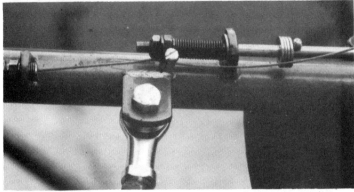

First step in throttle adjustment is finding a bottoming point. Some karts, such as the Yamahas, use a stop nut and bolt arrangement behind the gas pedal to limit movement. This Scorpion kart throttle rod bottoms out on the return spring. Without a stop, damage will result to the cable and the carburetor shaft.

Next, hold gas pedal wide open and push throttle shaft lever slightly to check for slack. Adjust cable by turning adjuster at carburetor and/or at the frame attachment.

Pencil points to low speed needle. Even though these needles are called "low and high speed," you can set the mixture mainly with the low speed. Tune the plug or exhaust color or temperature with the low speed. Recommended setting for a Yamaha is 7/8 of a turn out.

Pencil points to high-speed mixture adjuster. Recommended setting for a Yamaha is 3/4 of a turn out.

Idle adjustment screw. Be sure engine idles on its own as engine could die when you take your foot out of the gas to slow because most clutches do not provide engine braking.

is burning by looking at the color of the deposit inside the flex of your exhaust. The color should be dark gray to dark brown. White is too lean and you will burn a hole in the piston or seize the engine and if it is black, you will foul plugs and lose power.

**Chain Oiler.** Use a copper line at the end of the petcock, and then install a plastic line at the end of the copper tube. The plastic line can rub against the chain without any trouble and it can be pulled in or out easily to make up for chain movement after changing a gear. Fasten the plastic tube with a couple tie wraps. Cut the plastic line at an angle and let it rub against the gear. Centrifugal force will sling the oil on the chain. Any cheap oil can be used for the oiler. Some guys even reuse the oil they drained out of their

## Carburetor Nomenclature

*Courtesy of Yamaha*

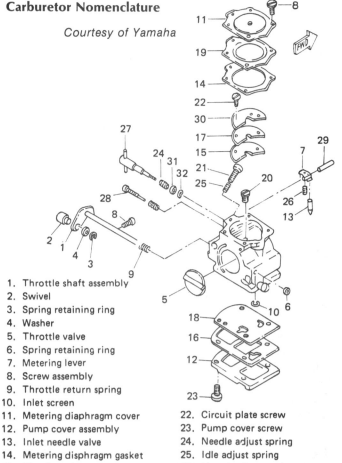

1. Throttle shaft assembly
2. Swivel
3. Spring retaining ring
4. Washer
5. Throttle valve
6. Spring retaining ring
7. Metering lever
8. Screw assembly
9. Throttle return spring
10. Inlet screen
11. Metering diaphragm cover
12. Pump cover assembly
13. Inlet needle valve
14. Metering disphragm gasket
15. Circuit gasket
16. Pump gasket
17. Circuit check valve diaphragm
18. Pump diaphragm
19. Metering diaphragm assembly
20. Metering lever pin screw
21. Idle adjust screw
22. Circuit plate screw
23. Pump cover screw
24. Needle adjust spring
25. Idle adjust spring
26. Metering lever spring
27. High speed needle assembly
28. Idle needle
29. Metering lever pin
30. Circuit plate assembly
31. Packing washer
32. O-ring

family cars.

Now is a good time to double check the mounting of the oiler. The oiler should be mounted to a secure surface with a good size bolt and lock nut or at least a lock washer. One of the five things that fall off karts most often is the oiler. The other four, by the way, are: exhaust system, ballast, number plates and air filters. Lose any one of those items and it could cost you a race or disqualification.

**Seat Mounting.** See the photos we have included in this book, showing correct seat mounting procedure. Run two bolts at the top of the seat mounts. If you use only one bolt, the mount will break at the weld. Give it a few races and it will happen for sure, especially in dirt or on a bumpy asphalt track.

**Exhaust Springs.** Install four springs at the flex, using the method shown in the photo. Use two springs at the canister part of the exhaust. Safety wiring the springs is a good idea.

**Nerf Bars.** If you run speedway, you definitely need the full length nerf bars. Mount them as shown in the photo. One slip tube at one end and a rod end at the other extremity will allow a loose fit and will not cause any frame binding. The slip tube should be a little larger than the end of the nerf being slipped in to allow for some play. Do not use the bolt-on type. You will never get them tight enough and the bars can hang down or slip if the nerfs get hit.

**Starter.** Charge the battery overnight. While you have the starter in hand, try it on. If you have installed wide nerfs or tires, the starter shaft may not reach all the way to the clutch. Your kart shop should have extensions for starters if the shaft is too short. Try moving the right rear wheel out a couple of inches, and see if the starter still fits. You may need that room someday — better be prepared now. You may find out at the starting line that you cannot start your kart because you moved the right rear out a few minutes before. Move the wheel back to where it was.

*Run a copper tube with an automotive petcock on the oiler. You can then add a plastic tube on the end of the metal tube and aim it directly at the chain or the gear.*

*Correct mounting of exhaust springs. Run safety wires through the springs for added safety.*

*Nice seat mounts on an Emmick kart. Struts are mounted with two bolts at the top to avoid lateral loading and stress at the weld on the bottom. Using just one bolt at the top, even for a few events, will result in a cracked mount.*

*Wide nerfs are necessary in speedway. Be sure yours are mounted loosely so they don't put a bind into the frame.*

*These bolt-on nerf bars are really handy. If you use clamps at both ends, tighten bolts very well or pin the bars on. The bars can slip and drag on the ground. It would be a good idea to slip one end of the nerfs into a butt tube of slightly larger size that was welded to the frame.*

**Double Check Clutch Oil.** If you use a wet clutch, of course. Here is an area where record keeping is very important. You may think that your buddy filled the clutch after he put it back together. You may think that you filled it, or you may not be completely sure you did. Make a note of when the clutch was filled and you will not have any problems. Follow manufacturer's procedures or, if you run a Horstman clutch, use the information we reprinted in this book. A word of caution about clutches. Do not tear out of the pits.

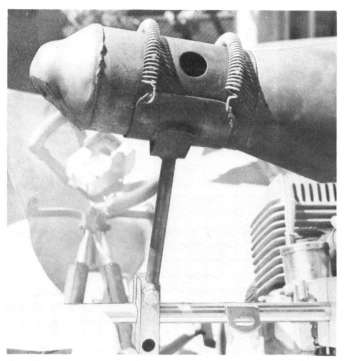

*Good way to support exhaust system. Run safety wire through the springs as a precaution.*

Accelerate slowly and allow the discs to grab before you give her full throttle. Also, if you spin out, take your foot out of the gas pedal, stop and accelerate off gently. Four or five wild spins will burn up a clutch if you don't take your foot out of it. You could also end up with a slipping clutch at the beginning of a race.

**Chain Adjustment.** Loosen the engine and exhaust system. Move the engine until the chain has about 1/4-inch of movement. Tighten the engine and double check the chain tension while turning the clutch through at least a complete revolution. Often the chain will not have the same

*To adjust or remove chain, loosen the two engine fastening nuts. The exhaust system should also be loosened. You should have already checked all the hoses and wires for adequate slack.*

*Chain should have about 1/4-inch of slack at its tightest point. Check tire to clutch clearance. Allow one inch minimum clearance or the tire will rub against the clutch in a left turn.*

system. Vibrations and centrifugal force will sometimes move the wires onto the exhaust. The result is a shorted plug wire and a stalled engine.

**Steering Wheel and Pedal Positions.** Turn the wheel all the way to the right and left while sitting in the kart. Are your arms fully locked at any time during the motions? If so, you are sitting too far back or the seat is leaned at too great an angle, or the steering is too high for your height. Make proper adjustments and remember to maintain correct weight distribution. Go back on the scales if necessary. Verify toe-in if you reset the steering height on the steering column. Depress the brake and throttle pedals. Are your feet fully extended and causing your calves to cramp? If so, adjust the pedals back or buy new ones. If your knees are up too high, you are probably sitting too far forward or the pedals are too far back.

*A short piece of key stock can be used to align the gears. Firmly hold the key stock against the driven gear and rotate axle to contact the key stock against the driving sprocket. Move the gear hub in and out of the axle until the key stock makes light contact with both sides of the driving gear.*

*Use a good ground on the engine kill switch. If you run nylon-lined rod ends and plastic steering shaft mounts, you will have to run the ground to another location. The nylon and plastic on the steering act as insulators.*

amount of tension all the way through the range. If the chain tightens as you turn the wheel, loosen the engine again and set the tension at the tightest spot. Secure the engine and exhaust system. Check the fuel line, throttle cable, and wiring to be sure they have enough play.

**Plug Wire and Temp Gauge Wire.** Run your plug wire and temp gauge wire lead, as shown in the photo. Tie-wrap the two wires together and run them away from the exhaust

*Run the plug wire and temp lead as shown here. This keeps the wires away from the exhaust.*

*Nice pedal set up on this Emmick kart.*

To check for steering bind, turn wheels to full lock and rotate tie rods between index finger and thumb. Turn wheels the other way and go through same process. Make necessary adjustments if either tie rod binds.

Correct tie rod set-up. Note use of washers, lock nuts and cotter pins.

(Left) If you do not have enough room to run a cotter pin, use some stainless steel wire. In this picture a safety lock nut is used.

Before installing tie rods, note how much thread you have to work with. Make a note of it in your track log book so you won't end up running out of thread on the rod ends. This is an important safety item that should be checked by inspectors along with thread quality. Be sure lock nuts are tight — pounding could tear the threads out of the rod or the bearing. Most kart manufacturers use different length rods on the right and left sides. If you use a short rod where a long one should be used, you will run out of thread or you will run dangerously low.

**Check Front End For Bind.** Turn the wheels all the way to the right and twist the tie rods. If one or both do not move, you have steering bind. Loosen one tie rod end, and readjust until there is some play in the tie rod. Tighten the rod ends and follow the same procedure with the wheels turned to the left. Do not turn the tie rods so much as to upset wheel alignment.

**Perform Your Own Tech Inspection.** Using the rule book from the racing association, go through your own tech inspection, and be very critical. Pay special attention to critical fasteners, and check safety wire and cotter pins. Check wheels for tightness. Check engine mounts and exhaust system.

**Check Chain Alignment.** You should have mounted the axle bearing on the engine side inboard, and with the longer side of the bearing facing the inside of the kart. If not you will not have enough room to move the gear hub in far enough to align the chain. Eyeball the chain for straightness, tighten the hub and spin the clutch through at least one revolution. If the chain catches on the front gear or does not turn freely, the alignment is off. Repeat this procedure until the clutch turns freely.

**Throttle Operation and Return.** Be certain there is no load on the cable when the pedal is fully depressed. See that the carburetor opens fully and returns freely. Hopefully you have installed an extra throttle return spring.

Pencil points to tie rod binding. This can cause tie rod breakage. The binding can be intensified by chassis flex. Do not leave this point to chance.

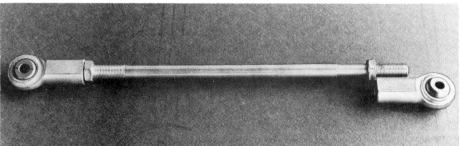

K&P's spindles are adjusted with shims. The track is set with spacers behind the hubs. Note excellent welding and gusset at spindle arm.

Run nylon washers on both sides of your front wheel bearings. The washers will keep dirt and moisture out without increasing drag.

**Choosing the Right Gear Ratio.** Gearing falls somewhat in the same category as reading tires in the sense that gearing is also an art that must be learned. In speedway some guys can show up at a new track, take a quick look at the track and guess their gear within a couple teeth. This ability comes with years of experience. Most of us have to rely on other methods to determine the correct gear to run on a particular track.

For speedway, I know of only three methods: Scientific, stopwatch and bogging.

**Scientific.** For using this method you will need a few tools: a tach, a stopwatch, a pocket calculator, and a horsepower curve of the engine/exhaust system you are running. You will probably have to beg or steal the horsepower curve. It would be easier to run your own dyno tests. Beginners do not need to get so involved, but this is the most accurate method of selecting the correct gear. Install the gear everyone seems to be running at that track and take a few laps. The exhaust should have been set about halfway through the manufacturer's range. On the track make mental notes of the lowest and highest RPMs encountered. The minimum RPM will be found as you start accelerating off the corner. The maximum will be at the end of the straight, just before you start braking for the turn. The key is to find the gear that will allow the RPMs to drop down to just below the peak power range. For example, if the power peak of your engine-pipe combination is 9,500 RPMs, the ideal gear will let you out of the turns at 9,300 to 9,500 RPMs. If the engine bogs coming off the turns, extend the flex about 1/4-inch to 1/2-inch until you come off the corner without any hesitation. This gear ratio will give you the lowest possible lap times. However, a beginner should use a larger driven gear because he will probably get stuck in traffic and get sideways more often than the more experienced driver. Both those situations cause a drop in RPMs. This method will work for a given track condition only. Try running that gear in the main and note lap times, tires used, track conditions, and weather. Your next time at that track, if the conditions are compar-

able, try a tooth or two either side of the ratio and note your lap times again. If times dropped, keep going in that direction until the times start going up. This method, unfortunately, requires several races to get dialed in. Keep accurate notes so if you go to a comparable track you will have some data to fall back on.

**Bogging Method.** This is the "seat of your pants" method. Install the gear recommended for that track in your class. Take a few laps and see if the engine "bogs" coming off the turns. The first indication of bogging is that you are getting passed coming out of a turn and you catch up again in the middle of the straights. You can also hear the engine bog. The exhaust sound will get deeper and lower than normal — the engine just doesn't "sing" like it should. If the engine bogs, try larger driven gears until the engine comes off the turns clean. If the engine does not bog and you are passing people coming off the turns, you might want to test a smaller driven gear, and keep decreasing the rear gear until the engine just starts to bog. At that stage increase the flex by 1/4-inch to 1/2-inch for really short tracks.

$$\text{Reduction ratio} = \frac{\text{Number of Driven sprocket teeth}}{\text{Number of Drive sprocket teeth}} = \frac{69T}{9T}$$

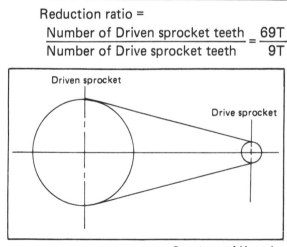

Courtesy of Yamaha

*The rear sprockets come in two halves that should be matched at the notches shown here. If you have an engraving tool, you might want to notch all four ends and scribe the number of teeth of that particular sprocket on all four sides. This will make things considerably easier at the track.*

**Stopwatch Method.** This method works best on asphalt tracks because conditions are almost perfectly constant. In contrast, a speedway track can change by the minute and take lap times along with it. Start with the gear recommended for that track in your class and take lap times. Next, install a larger gear, check lap times. Install a smaller gear and compare time with the large gear. Keep going in the direction that showed an improvement until you see an increase in lap times. Again, a novice should use a slightly lower gear than the fastest karts. In speedway, a slightly longer flex length will also be beneficial.

**Clutch Setting.** There is no real need to slip the clutch in speedway. However, in sprint you will get left behind if you don't slip the clutch coming off the slower corners. The clutch should be set to hook up just below the power peak. So if your engine puts out its maximum power at 9,250 RPM, set the clutch to grab at 8,800 to 9,100 RPM.

**Tuning the Exhaust System.** For speedway, the mid-to-low end of the range will usually work best. The pipe should be tuned to the gear, because the pipe is basically a fine-tuning device. For speedway, start at mid-range and increase the length in 1/4-inch increments, but only after you have found the fastest gear. Since fastest lap times will be recorded with the highest gear before the engine bogs, it is therefore advantageous to extend the pipe a small amount to give a clean launch off the turns and rely on the gear to keep the RPMs low in the power range. Remember that pipes differ in their power curves but they all follow one general rule: The longer the flex, the more bottom end power, and the shorter the flex is, the more power at the top end. This distance is measured from the side of the piston to the first weld, or from the face of the cylinder to the first weld on the chamber. A gain in power at either end of the power curve will show a loss at the other end. As a rule of thumb for speedway and slower sprint tracks, try to favor the bottom end because it is the area where you will find the most power and you will carry that speed all the way down the straight.

There are two more things to remember about pipe tuning. First, always keep all other set-ups the same when you are experimenting with the exhaust system. Otherwise, you will not know if the pipe or your other change has caused the variance in the lap times. Second, remember to reset the clutch (on a sprint kart), if you change the exhaust system or the flex length. If the flex has been shortened, you will have to slip the clutch more and make it grab at a higher RPM. If the flex was lengthened, one inch difference in flex length changes the power peak four to five hundred RPM.

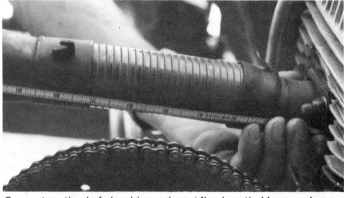

*Correct method of checking exhaust flex length. Measure from the side of the cylinder to the first weld on the pipe. Some pipe manufacturers give figures from the side of the piston to the first weld. In that case measure the distance from the side of the piston to the face of the cylinder and subtract that figure from the one given by manufacturer.*

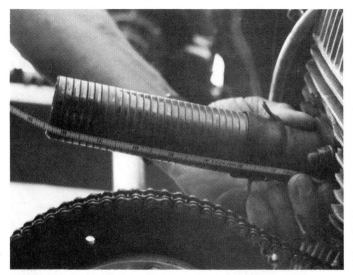

*Measuring the same piece of flex without the pipe, we find our measurement is about 1/4-inch less. The reason is that the cone extends into the end of the pipe by about 1/4-inch. Keep that in mind when measuring flex.*

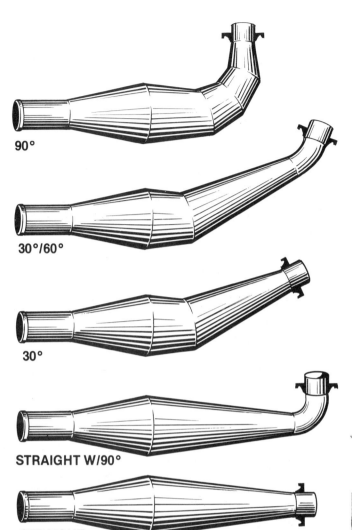

**90°**

**30°/60°**

**30°**

**STRAIGHT W/90°**

**STRAIGHT**

Exhaust systems come in several different angle configurations. The length and shape of each cone determine the power curve. The angles on the pipe have little effect on horsepower. (Courtesy of GEM Products)

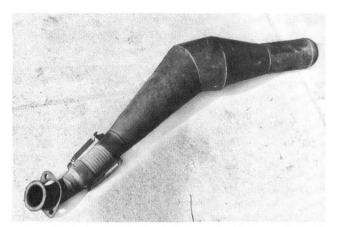

The Gary Hartman "200" pipe is the most widely used pipe in kart racing these days.

The Pitts Power pipe works best at 8-1/2 to 9-1/2 inches of flex from the face of the cylinder to the first weld on the pipe. The Power Pipe is a good all-around pipe and is recommended for beginners.

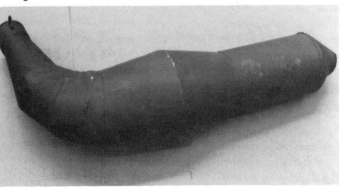

Gary Hartman's Blimp is still one of the best pipes around. This pipe works best at bottom end.

Do not use a flex with frayed ends like this. The ends could break off and end up in the engine. The pieces hanging off also restrict the flow of gases.

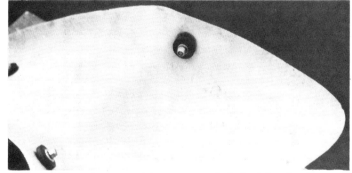

Mount fiberglass on rubber grommets to isolate vibration and prevent glass cracks.

## Pre-Race Checklist

Chain oiler full
Chain tension correct
Motor mounts tight
Axle bearings and circlips
Rear lugs
Steering links and bolts
Brake fluid
Brake pads
Front wheel bearings
Front lug nuts
Tire wear and pressure retention
Throttle linkage
Fuel line and filter
Wires
Other hardware and keys
Seat, floor, fairing
Exhaust system and springs
Clutch oil
Tools and accessories
Battery charged
Fuel mixed
Plugs
Safety equipment
Air filter
Number plates
All fasteners

## Tech Checklist

Steering wheel assembly and cotter pins
Wheels and bearings
Spindle nut and cotter pins
Toe rod ends and cotter pins
Steering support bolts and cotter pins
King pin bolt, nut and cotter pin
Steering support blocks
Pedals cotter pinned
Brakes operating properly and rods cotter-pinned
Brake calipers safety-wired
Axle snap rings on
Extra throttle return spring on
Exhaust secured
Brake caliper and master cylinder bolts cotter-pinned
Seat tight
Ballast mounted on frame, bolted securely and cotter-pinned
Numbers and number plates
Helmet
Gloves
Leathers or driving suit, other clothing or safety equipment
Sharp edges covered

*Brake calipers with shims should be safety wired. With heat, the shims could get loose and fall off, resulting in loss of brakes. Safety wire will retain the shims even if they get loose. Also note cotter pins and lock nuts on the caliper bolts.*

*Number plates can be fastened down with tie wraps. Tie wraps will facilitate removal and cleaning, and panels will not be as vulnerable to breakage.*

*These front mud guards are made with plastic pails. Ask your local hamburger or donut shop for a couple.*

This photo shows proper use of safety lock nuts on gear, axle bearing mount, oiler and exhaust manifold.

Use some type of "never seize" on your fasteners — especially on the nuts and bolts near the exhaust, hubs and any tapped aluminum.

Seat installation can be a real pain. Place a thin piece of wood or metal under the frame and clamp it with vise grips to hold the seat in place while you position it correctly.

(Left) Brake discs are drilled to increase cooling and reduce weight. However, drilling like this reduces the amount of brake swept area drastically, thus defeating the purpose. Grooved discs are much more efficient. They do not reduce braking area and still relieve pad gases created by the heat.

*This steering damper is a good idea for dirt tracks.*

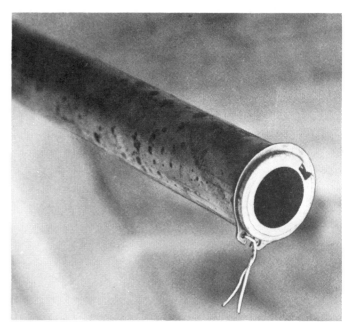

*It is a good idea to safety wire the circlip at the end of your axle. Position circlip opening opposite to key stock slot and tighten safety wire to prevent it from rotating on the axle. This should definitely be done if key stock slot is not welded shut at the end near the circlip.*

*It is a good idea to note tire pressure and diameter near the valve stem. This wheel is nicely mounted with nylon safety nuts backed with the correct size washers. Flange nuts are also nice to use because you don't have to hunt for the washers when changing tires at the track.*

# 7

# The First Race

As much as possible, load up and get everything done before the race, especially if it is a day race. Get your gas the day before (remember to mix in your oil, if you run a two-cycle). I like to use some kind of a tag or even a tied rag on the can to indicate whether I or someone else mixed in the oil. You will definitely ruin your engine if you run it without oil in your fuel. When loading up, use the handy checklist in this book.

Find out where to call to confirm if the race has been rained out. Even if the weather is nice and clear at your house it may be pouring cats and go karts at the track, or vice versa. I recently missed a race thinking it was raining at the track, fifty miles away, because it was pouring at home when I got up. I did not know where to call at 6 a.m. to find out if it was raining an hour's drive away. So I went back to sleep thinking we were rained out. By the same token, if you suspect it may have rained or may be raining at the track, contact somebody. You might call your friends in case they haven't read this book and they are assuming the race is on, or rained out.

Get to the track in plenty of time. Things are confusing enough your first time out. Give yourself plenty of time to register, unload, weigh in, set up ballast, paste numbers, etc.

Before you unload, go register and get your number. If you got there early enough you probably will luck out and get the number already on your kart. If not, you will have to change it. Most clubs give out numbers the first race of the season and you keep that number for the rest of the year. If you start racing during the season the club will still give you a

number but it probably will not be the number on your kart. If you race with more than one club you might have to use several numbers during the season. While at registration inquire about where the scale is located so you won't have to hunt around for it. Also find out the number of practice sessions, the order of races and qualifying heats, and where and when tech inspection is held. Another important point is to find out how your particular club holds its' qualifying. Some clubs use the "flying one lap" method.

You take one warm-up lap and one timed lap and the fastest qualifier gets on the pole, the slowest lap brings up the rear. After the qualifying they will have one or two "heat races." Usually the first four or six qualifiers are guaranteed that position for the main. The other guys have to race for their position and even if you win a heat you still will not get the pole (unless you were on the pole to start with). Doing well in qualifying is extremely important. A small track is difficult to pass on, and the further up in the pack you are the better your odds will be to finish well in the main.

Other clubs use qualifying heats. They will draw numbers for the start of the first heat. First heat will determine your starting position for the second heat. The second heat will determine your main starting position. Other clubs use two qualifying heats based on your registration time. First heat will be lined up in order of registration and the second heat is inverted; last registrants first and vice-versa. You score points "motocross style." The total number of points you score determine your starting position. Your club may use the draw method. Each driver draws a number

*Before: Getting up at 5 a.m. is fun . . . if you are going to the races.*

*After: If your pits are in the middle of the track, use caution while crossing to use the facilities. Never cross track during practice or a race.*

which determines his starting position in the first heat race. His finish in the first heat determines his position in the second heat, and the second heat finish determines the race starting position.

Now that you know the schedule, go weigh in with a dry tank. If you bring some ballast with you to the scale, you can add it right there and bring your weight up. Three or four pounds over is good insurance. If you are one of those people who can sweat five or ten pounds in a couple hours, add some extra weight before your races. It's a good idea to check your total weight exactly after each event. If you see you're losing weight during the event, add some more ballast. Do not count on gas or mud to amount to much. You might come in almost out of gas and by the main all the mud you had picked up in qualifying will have shaken loose.

Next, apply your numbers. If you do not have the numbers you need, use electrical tape. Remember that if the scorers cannot see your numbers they will not score you and that is the equivalent to a "no start." Some clubs will let you reserve numbers ahead of time, or they will sell numbers at the track.

Next fill out your track log form. The section in this book that has the log form will explain how to use the info and what everything means.

Start your engine in the pits and let it run for 30 or 60 seconds, with the low speed needle turned in (leaned down) a quarter of a turn. This will ensure that the plug is good and that you will not miss a start due to a fouled plug or other mechanical problem. Lean out the mixture until engine dies.

## Tech Inspection

Some clubs don't even have tech. Those clubs have more pieces falling off karts and more accidents than the clubs that do perform a tech inspection. Nevertheless, you should have done your own tech inspection.

*(Right) The correct method to weigh in. He has his helmet and gloves in the bag on his seat. He also brought some ballast to the scale in case he needs to bring his weight up to snuff, saving himself a trip back to the pits.*

## Drivers' Meeting

Attend it! You will get important information — upcoming events, new rules, new classes, safety items about the track, driving or tech tips. Some clubs also give out trophies for the prior race at the drivers' meeting. You will probably get some information on the schedule for the day, changes done to the track, holes in the surface, potential hazards, etc. In any case, attend the drivers meeting. You will probably learn something, and the information will make for a safer race.

## Practice

In speedway, the first practice is usually run on a muddy

track. Install at least four tear offs. A muddy condition will not help you in dialing-in your gear, pipe or handling. Chances are you and your kart will get completely covered with mud, which will have to be cleaned off before the next practice or race. Clean off your numbers first, without them you will not be scored. Take it easy. A muddy track is very slippery. Going slow and increasing your speed gradually will teach you much faster than going fast and spinning out every other lap. Do not bother timing yourself in the first practice. The only exception I can think of is a sand track that gets rewatered and groomed several times during the event. There the track should be about the same each time you go out on the track.

Practice is a good time to learn your lines. Try to follow the other drivers during practice and see how they drive. If you follow their lines, and if you have set up your kart using the guidelines we have given in this book, and if you use the pipe, gear and flex length recommended for that track, you should be right near the front.

If you run dirt, remember to turn on the oiler before you go out on the track and turn it off when you come back in the pits. When you turn off the oiler, see if the chain is well-lubed or if it is dry. If the chain is dry, one of three things happened: (1) The petcock was not open, or not open enough, (2) You ran out of oil, (3) The tube from the oiler moved away from the gear, or was never aimed properly. Remedy the situation and reset chain tension if it got loose from the lack of lubrication (remember to loosen the exhaust and retighten it when done).

In speedway, aside from maintenance and necessary repairs, I would not recommend you make any changes to handling, gearing, or pipe settings. What this will do is give you a feel for how different your lap times and handling will be as the track dries and hardens. A speedway track will get faster and faster as the event progresses. The reason for this is twofold: First, the track dries up and provides better traction, and second, the race organizers generally "move the

track in" as the races progress. Actually what they do is move the markers on the inside of the turns, which makes a shorter track with broader turns, thus faster lap times.

## Use The Restroom

Go to the restroom before going out on the track. There is an obvious reason for that, of course, but there is another reason most people never think of. If you get into an accident with a full bladder or intestines, and you get struck in the abdominal area, you might rupture the bladder or an intestine. That type of injury is very difficult for doctors to deal with. This type of injury is easy to prevent by following a very simple rule.

In speedway the track will get hard and dry on a hot night or during a dry day. "The blue groove" is where you want to keep your wheels or you'll end up in the tires or the wall in a hurry. One groove tracks are difficult to pass on.

Guys who bring these rigs to the track anticipate being asked for favors. If you can return the favor you will gain the respect of your fellow competitors and make new friends.

Some guys have all the luck.

*Correct method of installing tear offs. Alternate sides when placing another tear off, so when one is peeled off the end of the next will pop out on the other side, ready to be pulled off.*

## Between Heats

Check tire pressures each time you come in the pits, or go out on the track. Racing tires leak, slowly, but they leak. So double check the tire pressures after the tires have cooled down. Use a good quality gauge. The pencil-type gauge is fine for your family sedan, but for racing use a dial gauge with a pressure release valve.

## Refuel If Needed

Four to six inches of fuel in the tank should be enough for most speedway and sprint event. Experience will teach you how much fuel you will burn in a race. Always be on the safe side by using a bit more fuel in the tank than you think you may need.

## Oiler

See how much oil you have used. If you are down just a bit, refill next time. Use the end of a turkey baster to fill the oiler.

## Miscellaneous Checks

Check that number plates are securely fastened and free of dirt, go over exhaust fasteners and springs, see if chain needs adjusting, put an Allen wrench on the engine mounts, depress the throttle and verify you are getting full opening and that there is no bind on the cable (remember to

*A long funnel or . . .*

*. . . a piece of PVC pipe will facilitate tank filling, especially if you run a fairing.*

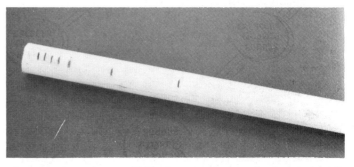

*Details of notches on PVC pipe used to pour fuel when tank is difficult to get to. Use the notches to gauge amount of fuel in the tank. Know how many ounces each notch is worth so you can determine your racing weight and how many laps you can go on the fuel you have left.*

check the throttle at least once at the track because the cable and its housing expand with temperature changes at different rates). Go over fasteners quickly, shake the mud off the air cleaner, do a visual inspection of safety wire and cotter pins, check wheels and spindle nuts. Check fuel lines and filter for bind and leaks at the connections. Check electrical connections and wires. All this should only take ten or fifteen minutes, unless you run into a problem. Pull the spark plug and inspect it. Replace it if needed and adjust the carburetor mixture. Wash your helmet and face shield. Use Windex or 409 and rinse with clear water. Replace tear offs.

## Qualifying

If your club uses the single timed lap method, the first thing to remember is to relax and take it easy. Go over the lap in your mind several times before going out on the track. Some guys try so hard during the single lap that they end up blowing the whole thing. If you run where they use the two-heat system based on your registration time, you may get a chance to start a race on the pole. However, I would recommend that your request starting in the rear in both heats your first couple of times out. Being on the pole is enough pressure for an advanced racer. Starting from the rear will give you a chance to learn driving in traffic, passing other drivers and being passed. When in doubt, don't pass. Remember you have plenty of time ahead of you without trying to prove anything in your first race. Again, if you have set up your kart the way we told you to, you will do a good job out there anyway.

If your club draws numbers for starting positions, use the same tactics and start in the back. You can bet nobody will protest you for giving them your spot. If you feel comfortable enough you might want to start in your earned position for the main. Again, if in doubt, start in the back and get the feel for things. You have more to gain than to lose.

## The Start

Races can be won or lost at the start. Small tracks are very difficult to pass on and the further up you start, the better your chances are to finish in front of the pack. A racer could be the fastest that night but if he starts in the middle or the rear of the pack, chances are he will only be able to pass one or two other karts per lap. Catching the other fast karts that started in the front will be next to impossible. Again, you are at your first race to learn. Watch the start of other races and learn where you should start accelerating so you won't be left behind or run over.

Find out what your starting position is before the start. Get up to the starting line or staging area in plenty of time. The start of the race just before yours is a good signal for you to get lined up. The white flag for that race will tell you to put on your helmet, gloves and elbow pad. After all the karts of the prior race have come in, turn on your oiler and get in

*At the start, the pole sitter should control the pack and set the pace. Here Number 6 is signaling, by raising his hand, that the starter wants another lap before he starts the race.*

your kart. Double check that your fuel is on and turn on your tach-temp gauge. Do not start your engine until you are instructed by the starter. If the engine is warm you may want to turn your low speed needle in a quarter turn or so. If the motor is cold, turn the needle out 1/8 to 1/4 turn. Reset the needle to determined setting after starting the engine.

When out on the track, get behind the guy who is starting in front of you and catch up to the leaders. If the kart in front of you has some kind of problem, just pass him. If he gets it back together he will catch up to you and pass you to get lined up for the start. If the leaders are way ahead of you it is your responsibility to catch up to them. The leaders are supposed to slow down to allow the guys in the back to catch up. Remember the number of the kart two karts in front of you. If the kart in front of you does not start you will know

*Hats off to all the scorers of the sport. They have to get up early on weekend mornings, stay up late on weeknights, devote their weekends, endure cold, heat, rain, sun, dust and mud. All that so we can officially enter a race and be scored.*

*In this picture Number 4 is approaching corner correctly. Number 98 is too far inside and will have to dart over abruptly to the left to approach the corner correctly. The last kart in the back should cut across track diagonally, thus using the least amount of track as possible.*

*Number 4 is entering turn correctly. The other kart shows correct exit line.*

*This kart is too wide off the turn. See photo above for correct line.*

which number to follow.

Let's pull out on the track and get lined up. Races seldom start on the first lap. The starter will want everybody bunched up good before he gives the green. Keep an eye on the kart on the pole. When you see him take off, start accelerating. Unfortunately, a start is usually like pulling on a chain; the front links move first and the rear pieces follow as they get pulled. The fellows in the back cannot pass until the green has fallen which means you have to follow the kart in front of you until the green is waved.

The green has appeared and you are going. Don't let all the noise and commotion mess you up. It's just as noisy and confusing for the other guys. Stay out of the way and don't look back. If a faster, more experienced driver wants to pass you he will. Do not change lines going down the straights, and use the "traditional" line in the turns. Let the other guys worry about passing you. If you are given the blue flag, give the inside line to your pursuer and wave him by so he knows it is safe to take your line into the turn. One last word: Go slower than you think you should go. In the heat of excitement you might get carried away and go into a turn too fast and lose it. When the checkered flag comes out, slow down and raise your hand. Proceed to the scales and weigh-in. You have just completed your first race.

After the event is over, look around and go over your checklist to be certain you have not forgotten anything at the track. Remember your starter! The starter usually gets taken to the pregrid and is left there for the duration of the event. It is easy to forget. When loading your kart after it has been run hard, watch out for the exhaust and the brakes — they'll be burning hot. I have gotten burned several times loading the kart up on the scale. I should have learned the first time.

*By the end of the race the pits can look somewhat chaotic. That's fine — it only means that you have been doing your work. If you find yourself with enough time to clean your tools and organize your pits, you are probably not doing all the work you should be doing in between heats. Remember to check your pits before leaving the track and see to it that you are leaving everything clean and tidy. Take a double look to be sure you have not left anything behind. If you have loaned or borrowed tools or parts, be sure the transaction has been reversed.*

## Between Heats Checklist

Tire pressures and possible leaks
Refuel
Oiler — refill and check operation
Electrical connections
Fuel lines and filter
Spark plug
Number plates — proper fastening and cleanliness
Throttle operation
Air cleaner — fastening and cleanliness
Exhaust springs and fasteners
Engine mounts
Fairing and other fiberglass
Clutch
Chain tension and lubrication
Carburetor mixture
Clean kart
Clean helmet and face shield
Install new tear offs
Enter info in the track log sheet

## Loading List (From Home Or The Track)

Kart
Stand
Tools
Spares
Pump
Air tank
Ballast
Starter
Lubricants and sprays
Suit, helmet, gloves, shoes
Tear offs
Log book
Stop watch
Gas (mixed)
Water
Food
Money
Tires
Funnel
Gears, pipes
Clipboard and pencils
License
Rags
Flashlight
Windex or 409
Fire extinguisher
Plugs
Tape
Wire
Ice chest
Checkbook
Membership card

## Before Going Out On The Track

All nuts and bolts
Tire pressures
Gas (and oil)
Chain adjustment
Engine tight
Oiler full and operating properly
Cotter pins
Axle snap rings
Play in front end
Go through track list
Wheels tight
Clutch oil
Tear offs
Mud off number plates and fairing,
Throttle operation
Exhaust
Ballast
Air filter

## Starting A Two Cycle

Be certain fuel shut-off is in the on position. If the engine is warm, lean the low speed needle ¼ turn (turn the needle in). If the engine is cold leave the needles alone. Open throttle halfway and have assistant install the starter and crank the engine over. If the engine does not start immediately, release the gas pedal and depress it all the way down immediately. Repeat this operation three or four times. If the engine absolutely refuses to start, check the following: 1) Plug — plugs tend to foul easily when starting the engine. If you have any doubts about the condition of the plug, replace it. 2) If new plug is installed and engine still does not fire up, remove plug and check for spark. If you have no spark, try another plug and check the spark before installing it in the motor. Also check if the motor and the TCI are grounded properly, check the rotor for ground and air gap. While the ignition cover is off, look for excessive moisture in that area. Look for broken or damaged wires and disconnect the kill switch if you have one. 3) Check fuel level and quality (is the fuel old, does it contain any water?) Is the fuel getting to the carb? Is the throttle opening?

If all the above checks out, the problem is probably inside the engine. The most common problem is a worn ring. Other problems could be: stuck piston, hole in piston, seized bottom end, or weak battery on starter. The needle in the carburetor will sometimes leak and cause a starting problem.

# 8
# Maintenance Between Races

As was said earlier, maintenance can be a real grind. The right tools and equipment will make things easier. A methodical approach will also help clarify things and prevent "I gotta do it overs." Make lists and use them. Know what you are going to do before the next race even before the last race is over. Figure out what parts you will need, and make a note of it on the track form. Determine and note if you will need a certain tool or piece of equipment you may need to buy or borrow.

The first thing you should do after a race is analyze your notes and see what needs to be done in terms of repairs, adjustments or modifications. Then transcribe those notes on a pad or a chalkboard. List all the operations you will perform and organize them in a logical order. This way you will not have to disassemble something twice. Plan on which day you will pick up the parts you need.

By analyzing your track notes first, you will be able to determine what needs to be modified and/or repaired. You may decide at that time to change the gear, exhaust, tires, seat position, etc.

Next, drain the fuel and refill the oiler. The reason you want to do those two things first is because those operations can get messy and you don't want to mess up a clean kart you just spent a half-hour cleaning. Put the gas in your family car. The oil will not bother it a bit. Watch that lead in newer cars — it could cause some problems.

Tie a rag or tag the gas can stating that there is no oil in the fuel yet. Remove the rag or tag as soon as you have mixed in the oil.

Clean up the kart. Use very low water pressure against the wheel bearings and the ignition box. Tie rod ends don't take too kindly to water and dirt either. Use a garden-type pressure sprayer with very hot water and a good laundry detergent. A mechanic's parts brush will do just fine to clean the tight spots, and those brushes are especially handy around the chain area. Cleaning your kart is an excellent

*I use this board in my garage for reminders, lists, parts shopping list and doodling new ideas. And, no, I can't read my handwriting either.*

Here is what happens when wheel bearings are not cared for. This bearing is frozen solid by rust and sand. The bearing was run on a dirt kart and the owner cleaned it with pressurized water. Pressure-forced moisture and dirt into bearing causing eventual failure.

Replace the front sprocket before teeth get this bad.

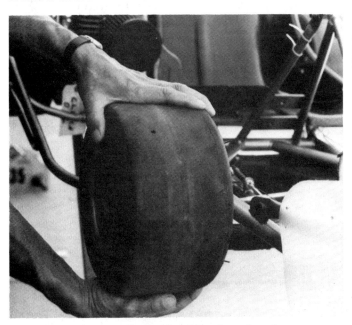

Between each race, check wheel bearings for play.

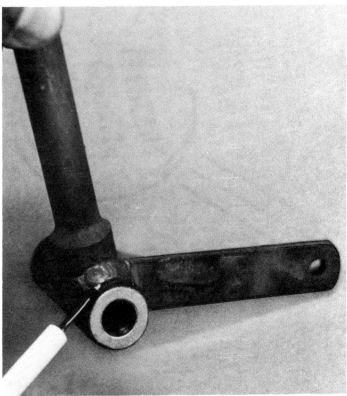

The weld on spindles should be checked periodically. Magnaflux or zyglo once a year.

opportunity to inspect for damage. Remove the rear wheels and clean the oil and grease of the inside halves. With the rear wheels off you will now have a clear shot at the chain and sprocket area. Spray the kart with compressed air.

When your machine is clean, it is a perfect time to go over it in detail. The following list will help you. Check front wheel bearings by spinning the wheels and check for any play in the bearing-kingpin area. Spin the rear wheels with the chain off. If you feel any grinding in the bearings, replace them. Check all welds, especially if you run speedway or on a bumpy asphalt track. Look at welds on the rear seat mounts — they are very vulnerable and should be paid close attention. Also look at the ballast mounts — they too tend to break. The fiberglass seats that come with most karts are prone to cracking. Inspect the fiberglass and repair any minor damage before it gets any worse. The most vulnerable areas are around the edges and between the shoulder blades.

Take a close look at the fuel lines and the carburetor pulse hose. Are the lines old and cracked or getting hard? Are they getting discolored? Are the clamps tight? Look for signs of leakage, dirt near the connections or wetness at the clamps. Look at the fuel filter. Is it dirty? And is it safety fastened?

Check the electrical system. Is the plug wire away from the exhaust system? Do wires and hoses have enough slack to move around, and could the engine be moved forward without putting any bind on them? The tach and temp gauge wires should be run separately to avoid any interference.

Look at front sprocket. Check for tooth wear. If the teeth are sharp and pointed, the gear should be replaced.

Check engine mounts for tightness. You will need to loosen the mounts to adjust the chain, change the gear or the front hub. Tighten mounts after replacing gears or chain.

Replace your gear as dictated by the track notes. While the engine is loose replace the exhaust flex if necessary. Remember that some pipe manufacturers quote the flex pipe length from the side of the piston to the beginning of the first cone in the expansion chamber. The port of a Yamaha engine measures about two inches. So, subtract two inches from the figure and you should be right there. Use a spring hook to reinstall the exhaust springs. Using one of those tools will save you many a bleeding finger. Note any changes in your new race log sheet for next race. Look at the color of the inside of the exhaust flex. That color will indicate how well the mixture is set. White is too lean, screw low-speed needle out about 1/8 of a turn. Black means too rich,

*Pencil points to an area that should be inspected periodically. The welds on these seat strut mounts often crack. Be certain you have two bolts at the top of the strut, or the weld will crack for sure.*

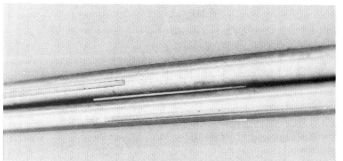

*To check axle for straightness, set doubtful axle next to good axle and check for gaps with a piece of paper. Now would also be a good time to check for cracks down the key way.*

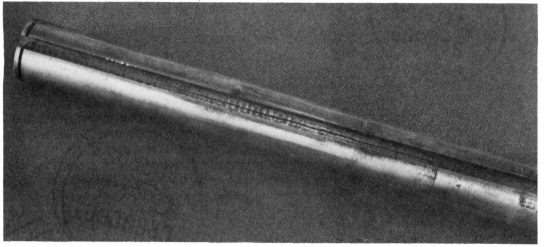

*This axle had a piece of key stock installed in it which was too wide for the axle groove. This crack was the result. The key stock was then loose and could have caused a wheel to fall off because the end of the axle key way was not welded at the snap ring.*

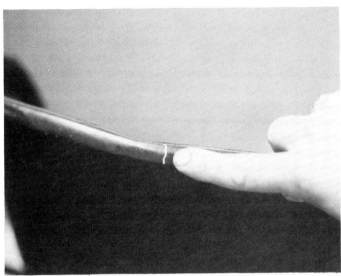

*Look for cracks in the back of your seat. If your seat needs repair, you can get fiberglass kits from large hardware or paint stores.*

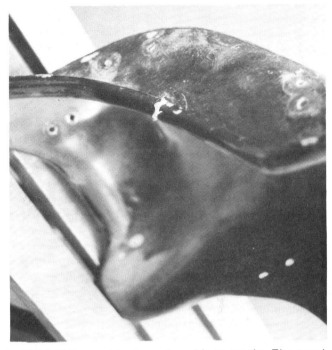

*The "hip" of the seat is also vulnerable to cracks. The possibility of cracks is another reason not to anchor the carburetor return spring to the seat.*

*When checking compression, always ground the spark plug wire. To get accurate reading open throttle all the way. Check compression after installing new ring and/or piston. Make a note of the reading, so you can have a base figure to work from when you check the compression in between races. The engine needs work if compression has dropped more than five pounds.*

screw needle in about 1/8 of a turn. Dark gray or chocolate brown is perfect.

Remove the air filter and inspect it. Even in speedway you will not need to clean it every race, unless you run on a very dirty and/or muddy track. Follow manufacturer's recommendations for cleaning and oiling, and use manufacturer's recommended oil.

Remove the spark plug and inspect it. Some guys replace their plug before each race. I don't think that is necessary. Replace the plug every four or five races. If the ceramic is black, go to a hotter plug. If the ceramic is parched white or blistered, go to a colder plug.

While the plug is out, check compression, following instructions given earlier. On a stock Yamaha you should have 110 to 120 pounds of compression. Good motors will put out 115 to 125 pounds. If you use a compression gauge with the fitting you screw into the spark plug hole, you will register a few more pounds. If your motor puts out 110 pounds or less, pull the head, cylinder and piston. Refit the piston and ring to the cylinder or have an experienced engine builder reassemble the powerplant. The throttle must be fully open when checking compression or you will get a false reading.

Check the carburetor opening and closing. Look for bind in throttle cable and see if it opens fully. Inspect throttle return springs.

Brake pads should also be inspected periodically. Look for cracks, uneven wear, excessive wear or burning. Remember the safety wire and the cotter pins when reinstalling calipers. If you got the brakes really hot, or you are reassembling them, you should bleed the whole system. Refer to the manufacturer for proper method of bleeding the system. Brake fluid should be replaced at least twice a year. Flush the system with a fluid recommended by the manufacturer and refill with correct fluid. Rebuild the whole system once a year. Check brake lines for cracks, crimps, chafing, etc.

Read your tires. Again this is somewhat difficult for a beginner to do, but you will have to learn sooner or later. If you know someone who is more experienced and can coach you, do seek his advice. Tire manufacturers are the best source of knowledge. Hopefully you have enough wheels to keep all the tires you need on hand without having to dismount the old tires every time. Splitting rims is probably the most hated job in karting. For breaking the bead, don't even bother trying to dismount the tires without a bead breaker. You will ruin a tire and lose your cool. If you need a tire breaker on an occasional basis, ask your kart shop if they would mind letting you use theirs (or have them do it).

Check front end alignment. Reset if necessary. Follow instructions in chapter on "setting up the kart."

Adjust the ballast if you are going to run a different weight class next time out. If you noted what your weight was at the last race, you will know exactly how much weight to shift. Ballast should be checked even if you do not need to change it. The mounting bolts can work loose. Use nylock nuts and safety wire whenever possible.

If you are going to race at a different track next time, you may need to change the numbers on your kart. Do not replace the number each time. Just purchase additional plates and install the other numbers you will need. Now when you return to that track, all you need to do is replace the plates. Keep some spare numbers on hand anyhow. They tend to peel off when the kart gets washed, and they get scraped off by other karts when they get a bit close to you in a race.

Check the front end for play, and check tie rods for bind with the wheels turned in both directions. Place the kart back on the scales to check for any frame misalignment. Now you can be sure your starting base is still the same. Charge the battery for your starter overnight, the night before the race. Check battery water level on occasion. If you use an automotive battery, run it in your car every so often; batteries get more wear from setting than from regular use.

Wash your driving suit. Chances are you have oil, grease, sweat, dirt and make-up from the trophy girl all over it. Also clean your helmet and visor. Replace tear offs with new ones.

Get a new race log sheet ready for the next race. Include any changes and modifications you have performed. Write down anything you may need to remember then, such as new gear, pipe, or flex length you will want to try. Strategies can be noted now that you have a clear mind and that you don't have any pressure on you from the race.

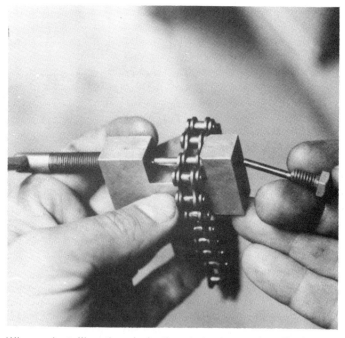

*Chain breaking is easier with the breaking tool in a vise, but at the track the hand method usually prevails. Tighten handle until pin has passed through the link.*

*When reinstalling the pin in the chain, insert the aligning pin through the back of the tool to align the link with the pin.*

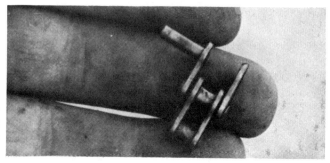

*Leave one pin in the link and one in the chain. Simply press pin remaining on chain back in to complete loop. It is good insurance to peen the pin with a sharp punch and hammer, but that is sometimes difficult to do at the track.*

# 9

# The Four Cycle Classes

For a youngster, the "Rookie" or "Junior" four cycle classes are an excellent entry level into karting. Speeds are relatively low, costs and upkeep are minimal and the competition is stiff and spirited in all the classes. It is not unusual in some parts of the country to have thirty or forty four cycles show up at a particular race.

A well-built "Briggs" engine should last a couple of seasons before a rebuild, and the knowledge required to operate the little four banger is very limited. Fifty dollars should cover the parts and lubricants for the rebuild, and since very little machining is allowed on these motors, that cost is virtually eliminated.

Should the karter desire more speed, he can run the dual engine, modified, or open classes. The "open" classes allow just about any modifications except for supercharging, fuel injection or aluminum flywheels. These motors can really run into money and the upkeep is relative to the increase in power. The "Briggs" for instance, was designed to turn 2 or 3 thousand RPM but after modifications and the use of alcohol the little "tater digger" can wind up to 7,000 RPM.

The "Briggs and Stratton" is by far the most widely used engine in four cycle, but Honda, Kawasaki and Tecumseh are also used in certain parts of North America. Check what is being run in your area before buying an engine or you might be stuck traveling long distances to find a track that runs your motor.

## Basic Stock Class Rules

The rules for the stock classes are very simple: you can't

*The great cost cutting feature of the four cycle class is that the Briggs engine is very durable and reliable, plus easy and inexpensive to work on.*

do anything! Unfortunately to be competitive and to remain legal, much must be done or at least checked. Legality will be the concern in this chapter. If you have an eye toward performance, seek the services of a competent engine builder. If you have any doubts about a certain modification check the rule book, ask an engine builder or an official, and then if you are still in doubt — don't.

**THE CHAIN GUARD: SAFETY FIRST.** Use a good chain guard — the thicker the better. A broken chain at 7,000 RPM will sling out with the force of a small bullet and it can break an arm or at least cause severe lacerations to the shoulder.

Many four cycle racers are very professional in their approach to the sport. These lads ran the "Noram" series with two karts.

A strong chain guard is not just a good idea, it is a rule. Remember that a chain can cause severe injuries to a driver's shoulder if it should break. Two cycle clutches must be run dry on four cycles.

The use of a chain guard is strictly enforced and with just cause.

**THE AIR CLEANER.** A good air cleaner is a necessity especially if you are going to run in the dirt. The rules allow for any air cleaner that is safely mounted. The "K&N" air filter can be used in conjunction with the Yamaha kart engine filter mount. The "K&N" filter is the most practical, most efficient and it provides the least amount of air flow restriction of any air filter on the market.

**CRANKCASE BREATHER AND OIL CATCH CAN.** Stock crankcase breather #294178 must be used in all the stock classes and it must be unaltered. A hose may be attached to lead the spewed oil into a catch can which is also mandatory.

**LEGAL ENGINES.** Only the following engine numbers are legal in the stock classes: 130202, 130232, 132223.

**INTERNAL ENGINE RULES.** Bore, stroke, valve springs and keeper dimensions camshaft timing, combustion area, head gasket, carburetor, piston, rod, and many other parts are subject to specifications. Taking the measurements involved requires accurate measuring tools and the job should be left to a competent engine builder. The engines in the four cycle classes are not built specifically for karting and karting rules are the furthest thing from the manufacturer's mind when designing and building these powerplants. That is why some parts are illegal straight from the factory. Because of this a karter, even if he is not performance oriented, should check his engine against the rules.

**GAS TANK.** If the right rear wheel on a Briggs is to be run all the way in, the gas tank will need to be notched to allow the tire to fit under the tank. This modification is legal and should be done by a qualified welder. Allow the tank to soak in soapy water for a few minutes and then flush it out completely before welding. Gas fumes explode more easily than liquid gasoline and some welding shops will refuse to work on gas tanks for that very reason.

The stock gas cap must be used.

**ENGINE COVERS.** Engine sheet metal covers must remain intact. These shields provide better cooling by routing the air flow in the correct patterns. The recoil cover may be removed. Some karters perfer to remove the recoil cover because a hit on the side could push the cover into the flywheel fins and broken fins are not legal, unless caused by a hit sustained during that day of racing.

**GOVERNOR ASSEMBLY.** The governor assembly must be removed.

**ROOKIE RESTRICTOR PLATE.** The restrictor plate (manufactured by Horstman) must be used by all "Rookies." This plate is designed to slow down the pace and provide safer racing for the young ones.

**ENGINE STARTING.** Starting a four cycle alky motor can be a real pain. The first thing to watch is not to overchoke the engine. Pull the choke out and crank her over once. If the engine does not fire the first time, reset the choke back in and crank her up a few more times to clean up the plug. Plugs foul easily with alky. If the motor did not fire up on your first attempt, try again, holding the throttle about halfway.

**EXHAUST PIPES.** The straight pipe is always a good standby. Sophisticated megaphones may work better under certain conditions but the novice should stick with the basics. Plug the pipe with a rag or a cork after running the motor. Plugging the pipe will prevent cold air from entering

Corking the exhaust pipe will prevent cold air from entering the engine and causing a possible bent or cracked valve. This will also prevent dirt and small objects from entering the combustion chamber.

Oil fill plug. Briggs' are equipped with two of these plugs, one at the front of of the engine, as shown, and one at the rear. Bottom of photo shows the oil drain plug.

the combustion area and possibly warping a valve. This will also prevent any debris from entering the engine via the exhaust.

The bolts securing the exhaust to the motor often back out with heat and vibrations. To prevent losing the exhaust, clean the threads and reinstall the bolts with "Loctite" and safety wire them. Use the same procedure on the carburetor bolts.

If you find it difficult to get to the lower carburetor flange bolt, use a ¼" Allen head bolt and cut an Allen wrench down to about ¾".

**OIL.** Most engine builders recommend a 20/50 or 30/50. Synthetic oils are very popular and seem to burn cleaner. If you run alcohol, the oil must be changed after each and every race. To change the oil, loosen the plug at the base of the engine. The oil is poured back in by one of the two plugs provided on the left side (clutch side) of the engine. Fill to the base of the threads on the plug hole. The engine must be level, so if you run a 15 degree angled mount you will need to tilt the whole kart back 15 degrees. Replace the oil ofter each race especially if you live in a humid area.

**ALCOHOL.** Keep in mind as a safety precaution that alcohol burns without a flame and only heat waves are visible when alky is ignited.

The alcohol must be drained out of the tank and the carb before storage because alcohol eats up rubber and aluminum. Refill the tank with pump gas and run the engine for a few minutes. The carb is probably set up very rich to run with the alcohol, so you might want to install a really hot plug or turn in the mixture screw.

The main jet should be drilled out to .48 or .50 for use with alcohol and the mixture screw should be run 2 or less turns on alky. Run 1¾ to 2 turns on gas.

No additives are allowed in the alcohol (or gas, for that matter). This rule is subject to electronic meter testing and laboratory testing.

The oil must be changed after each and every race as the alky contaminates the oil.

Use a Champion J4J or J6J spark plug and gap it to .023 to .026.

**VALVE ADJUSTMENT.** The question always comes up: "How do you adjust the valve?" The only way to adjust the valves is by sinking them into their seat by grinding. This should be done while doing a valve job and the operation should only be attempted by someone with the knowledge and tools necessary for the task.

**CLUTCHES.** Rules specify a dry clutch only. The clutches on four cycles are mainly used to get out of the pits so the settings are not very critical. Generally four cycle clutches can be run straight out of the box without any need of adjustment.

**CHAIN.** Spray the chain with a chain lube before each heat. A well lubed chain will be easier on the gears and it will require less power from the engine.

Center right of this photo shows the mixture adjustment screw. At left is the oil breather can, a mandatory piece of equipment to prevent oil drips on the track. Top shows good method of mounting the air filter. Note the nasty marks left on the tank from the alcohol.

# 10
# Record Keeping

Almost every chapter in this book has mentioned that it is important to record every change that you make to your kart. Now I'll remind you of that and tell you that it is important to keep records for every phase of your racing operation. I'll be the first to admit that record keeping is somewhat less than exciting, much less than setting records. But the two go hand-in-hand. Taking the time to keep accurate, detailed records will allow your racing effort to be efficient and more successful.

Keeping records will allow you to achieve a higher level of performance by:

1. Knowing which changes to make to your car for specific conditions
2. Improving reliability
3. Allowing you to make systems changes using good judgment based on real data
4. Saving time
5. Increasing confidence

Keeping records will allow you to increase the safety factor of your racing by:

1. Keeping an accurate and periodic check on vital components on your car
2. Minimizing "rush" work to make a race
3. Nearly eliminating "forget to do it" statments by your crew

4. Knowing when to replace or test (Magnaflux, Zyglo) vital parts
5. Knowing everything is done

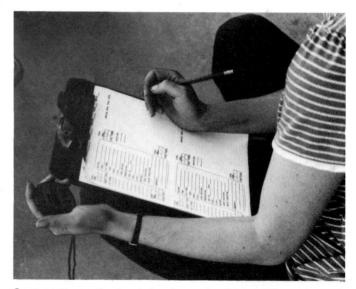

*Comments on the track log form should be entered immediately after driver has returned in the pits. Crew person should have noted lap times while kart was out on the track.*

Keeping records will reduce the cost of your racing by:

1. Winning more prize money by finishing more races
2. Utilizing time more efficiently
3. Minimizing needless crashes from parts failures
4. Knowing where problem areas are and what changes are necessary to overcome them.
5. Eliminating duplicated effort or non-effort

All of the factors that save money, increase safety and performance also save time—lots of it. Take a little time to save a lot of time and money.

Keeping records falls into these general areas:

1. Bookeeping: From tires to travel to power bills.
2. Travel plans: Advanced plans to save hassles.
3. Parts inventory: So you have what you need when you need it.
4. Maintenance schedule: So what needs to be done gets done on time.
5. Check Lists: So you don't forget to do things and take equipment and spares to the races.
6. Chassis and engine specs and part numbers.
7. Testing: Dyno, track, skid pad and aerodynamic.
8. What you do at the races.
9. Track information.
10. Work schedules: Who does what, where and when.

It all sounds like a lot of work. It is. But the effort will save time and money, and increase the level of performance and safety. All of these things are important to us.

*A good track log form.*

# Summary

We just took you from A to Z. From a total novice to a knowledgeable beginner. The difference is about a year of racing experience.

Unfortunately the motor racing alphabet has no end to its letters. The day Mario Andretti won the world championship, he had reached his Z for that season. However, the next day was back to point A for Mario. Every race is an alphabet of its own, only concluded at the checkered flag. Each time a driver changes class or form of racing, each new event, each new change is back to point A. New set-ups to try, new tires to test, new aerodynamics, new cars to develop.

The recent switch to turbo power in Formula One is a typical example of going back to point A. In 1983 teams without turbos were at point X, Y, or Z, but in the prior year's alphabet.

Motor racing is a never-ending stream of research, development, testing and frustration. A car can be the fastest this race and not even make the field the next day.

The readers of this book will soon learn that nobody has all the answers. Whoever is the most correct, in a particular race, wins. The late Jim Clark once said that racing was a game of mistakes and he who makes the least number of mistakes wins. One need not know everything in a motor race. Nobody does anyway. But at a given race if one competitor knows more than the other racers on the track that day, he will win, assuming he has comparable equipment. Knowledge is the ever-dividing factor. Simply put: The front runners have knowledge the other guys do not have.

Knowledge comes partly from asking questions, listening, and observing. But reading will provide you with data at your fingertips. Literature is other men's minds put in the palm of your hand. Their knowledge at your reach. Read everything you can that is related to racing — directly or indirectly.

Experience provides a very special form of knowledge. Bits of information stored in your subconscious that can be drawn out of your mind without thinking or calculating. You no longer react — you respond to the environment.

In a sport where milliseconds can spell victory or defeat, even life or death, it is essential to have what is often called a sixth sense. Whether you continue racing karts on a small scale or move your way up to the big cars, you will see this sixth sense at work. From a decision to change tires, all the way to deciding between a turbo or a non-turbo machine. All this intuition is based on knowledge so deeply rooted into your subconscious that decisions now appear instinctive.

Graham Hill once said that motor racing cannot be taught and any driver who claims he can explain how to race a car is not a good driver. What he really meant was that a driver or mechanic does not have the time to sit and think about the next move. Every movement is first rehearsed in the mind and then executed by the body. Look at a golfer swinging his club. He uses hundreds of muscles, each one at a very definite moment, all in a flowing, accurate motion. The swing lasts less than a second and the brain has to control all those muscles at precisely the right instant. The swing is performed in the mind first and then executed by the body. The swing motion has become subconscious. The same principle prevails in racing, be it driving the car, repairing it or setting it up for a certain track.

We sincerely hope this book has been a good starting guide for you. Follow our advice and instruction which came from other beginners' experiences. This book contains knowledge that would have taken at least a year of racing to learn. Use it wisely, and "good racing."

# Suppliers Directory

## Kart Shops And Accessory Dealers

**American Power Sports**
12300 Kinsman Rd.
Newbury, OH 44065
(216) 564-8100

**APPCO**
5839 Hamilton-Middletown Rd.
Middletown, OH 45324
(513) 539-9900

**Burris Racing**
10661 Humboldt St.
Los Alamitos, CA 90720
(310) 493-2031

**Franklin Motorsports**
8005 S. 13th St.
Oak Creek, WI 53154
(414) 764-1884

**G.E.M. Products**
496 E. St. Charles Rd.
Carol Stream, IL 60188
(708) 653-1800

**Grid Line Kart Shop**
9555 Barlow Trl. NE
Calgary, AB Canada T3J 3C5
(403) 250-1717

**Griffith Specialties**
510 Waterman Dr.
Harrisonburg, VA 22801
(540) 433-2408

**Jim Hall Kart Racing School**
1555-G Morse
Ventura, CA 93003
(805) 654-1329

**John's Kart Shop**
7049 W. Archer Ave.
Chicago, Il 60638
(312) 586-5600

**K & P Manufacturing**
950 W. Foothill
Azusa, CA 91702
(818) 334-0334

**Kart World**
1488 Mentor Ave.
Painesville, OH 44077
(216) 357-5569

**Le Circuit Du Karting**
160 Cine Parc
Mt. St. Hilaire, PQ Canada J0H 2G0
(514) 584-3843

**Margay Products**
3233 S. Kingshighway
St. Louis, MO 63139
(314) 771-4242

**Pfau Distributing**
1510 N. Alberta St.
Portland, OR 97217
(503) 283-1026

**Pitts Performance**
7922 Woodley
Van Nuys, CA 91406
(818) 780-2184

**Silver King Power Sports**
2500 South 2300 West, Suite 21-B
Salt Lake City, UT 84119
(800) 866-4631

**T.S. Racing**
123-C W. Seminole Ave.
Bushnell, FL 33513
(904) 793-9600

**Target Distributing**
19819 Orchard St.
South Bend, IN 46637
(800) 348-5076

## Manufacturers

**Briggs & Stratton Motorsports**
P.O. Box 702
Milwaukee, WI 53201
(800) 276-0765

**Comet Kart Sales**
2650 W. Main
Greenfield, IN 46140
(317) 462-3413

**Competition Karting,Inc.**
9 Austin Lane
Welcome, NC 27374
(704) 731-6111

**Emmick Enterprises**
5877 Power Inn Rd.
Sacramento, CA 95824
(916) 383-2288

**K & P Manufacturing**
950 W. Foothill
Azusa, CA 91702
(818) 334-0334

**Nelson Manufacturing**
994 S. First St.
San Jose, CA 95110
(408) 293-3702

**Sox and Son**
2223 Platt Springs Rd.
West Columbia, SC 29169
(803) 794-7247

**Trick Karts**
Tubular Resources Inc.
18518 Statesville Rd
Cornelius, NC 28031
(704) 896-8279

**White Chassis Racing Karts**
10246 Old National Rd.
Indianapolis, IN 46231
(317) 838-9133

## Karting Publications

**The Inside Track**
1800 W. D St.
Vinton, IA 52349
(319) 472-4763

**Karter**
4650 Arrow Hwy,. Suite B-4
Montclair, CA 91763
(909) 625-5497

**National Kart News**
51535 Bittersweet Rd.
Granger, IN 46530
(219) 277-0033

**World Karting**
5725-D Hwy 29 N
Harrisburg, NC 28075
(704) 455-1606

## Karting Associations

**IKF**
4650 Arrow Hwy., Suite B-4
Montclair, CA 91763
(909) 625-5497

**WKA**
5725-D Hwy 29 N
Harrisburg, NC 28075
(704) 455-1606